John's love for people and wholehearted passion for the local church to thrive have caused him to capture a message that will unlock potential, purpose, and clarity within every reader. He shares of God's endless, revolutionary, and profound grace, a grace he has been so evidently marked by in his decades of pastoring and leading. You are about to embark on a rich and life-changing journey to discover the depths of God's miraculous grace, and you have no greater guide than my friend John.

—BRIAN HOUSTON
GLOBAL SENIOR PASTOR, HILLSONG CHURCH

This book is like Beethoven meets beatboxing! It's very well written—replete with interesting anecdotes about church history and deep theological truisms—but it's also incredibly practical and life-giving. It's less about *exegeting* the concept of divine grace and more about *experiencing* the tangible compassion of God, actually leaning in to His miraculous, shame-eviscerating, unmerited, transformative kindness—which is why *Soul Set Free* will be on my nightstand for a long, long time!

—LISA HARPER
SPEAKER AND AUTHOR, *THE SACRAMENT OF HAPPY*

Far too many followers of Jesus feel trapped by their past, enslaved by their failures, and defined by their faults, which is why I can't wait for people to read *Soul Set Free*! Grasping the enormity of God's grace and its transformative power can change everything about the way you live life and walk with God. Everyone needs to read this book!

—MARK BATTERSON
*NEW YORK TIMES* BEST-SELLING AUTHOR, *THE CIRCLE MAKER*
LEAD PASTOR, NATIONAL COMMUNITY CHURCH

Pastor John has spent his entire adult life loving Jesus with his family, leading one of America's greatest churches, and learning the heart of God by preaching every verse of the entire New Testament, along with much of the Old Testament. Many of us have been long awaiting this book from one of this generation's greatest Bible teachers. This message on the grace of God is the gist of the gospel and a gift to the church. I am purchasing multiple copies to give away and encourage you to do the same.

—Mark Driscoll
Founding and Senior Pastor, The Trinity Church,
Scottsdale, Arizona
President, Mark Driscoll Ministries
Author, *Spirit-Filled Jesus*

Being a Christian isn't about following rules. It's about freedom—the freedom we have in Christ to pursue a truly abundant life. John Lindell's *Soul Set Free: Why Grace Is More Liberating Than You Believe* is a powerful journey into God's overflowing compassion and forgiveness. It's the spark you need to ignite a new passion for the overwhelming love God has for you.

—Craig Groeschel
Founding Pastor, Life.Church
*New York Times* Best-Selling Author

I am thrilled that John Lindell has written his first book! This insightful Bible teacher has given us *Soul Set Free: Why Grace Is More Liberating Than You Believe*, and it will be a huge help to everyone who reads it. John's teaching about God's grace outlines the vast treasury of blessings we have in Jesus Christ and that so many of us miss out on. Get this book in your hands, and you will find just how liberating the grace of God can be in your own life.

—Jim Cymbala
Senior Pastor, The Brooklyn Tabernacle

Most followers of Jesus know that God's grace is central to their relationship with Him, but they don't always grasp the extent of His liberating power in their lives. In *Soul Set Free*, John Lindell unlocks the chains of misunderstanding, shame, and frustration that keep many people from walking in the power of the Lord. Grounded in God's Word and filled with practical examples, this book will transform your understanding of amazing grace!

—Chris Hodges
Senior Pastor, Church of the Highlands
Author, *The Daniel Dilemma* and *What's Next?*

In a world where many may struggle to believe that God could really love us in our brokenness, this book is a refreshing reminder of the infinite grace that is ours in Christ Jesus. Lindell takes readers on an important journey in the Book of Romans that culminates with the panoramic view of God's work for us on the cross, God's work in us through His Spirit, and God's work with us in grace. This book is a handy companion in a world of condemnation and rage with a central message: God is for us!

—ED STETZER
BILLY GRAHAM DISTINGUISHED CHAIR, WHEATON COLLEGE

The truth contained in this book could radically change your life. You may be familiar with the term *grace*, but have you been plunged into the depth of freedom promised through the grace of God? You are holding a road map; dive in.

—SHEILA WALSH
AUTHOR, *IT'S OKAY NOT TO BE OKAY*

It's one thing to write about grace, but it's entirely different to live it out. Pastor John is a man who embodies the Word not just on platform but in everyday life. This book has opened my eyes, as a church planter and Bible teacher, to the power—as Pastor John says—that *grace* changes everything. Through his wisdom I'm learning how to live and lead with an extra measure of grace in my congregation, my marriage, and my family.

—BIANCA JUAREZ OLTHOFF
BEST-SELLING AUTHOR, BIBLE TEACHER,
PASTOR, THE FATHER'S HOUSE OC

Reading this book feels like a conversation with John, and those conversations have blessed me big time through the years. *Soul Set Free* is classic John Lindell—an inspiring and encouraging, yet practical, word that you can plug right in to your life. No matter what season you are in, this book will find you. John's masterful expository on grace makes for a power-packed narrative of what it truly means to be a son or a daughter of God. *Soul Set Free* embodies what it means to live a life of true freedom that Christ gave us. The practical, powerful tools John lays out in these eighteen chapters will change your life. This book is challenging and life-giving, all while extending an invitation to better understand God's heart for you.

—JEREMY FOSTER
LEAD PASTOR, HOPE CITY CHURCH

*Soul Set Free* helps you see why grace is so often called "amazing." From his own experiences in life and from his exposition of Romans, Pastor John clearly reveals how this one-syllable word, grace, is not only a distinguishing feature of the gospel but is what sets Christianity apart from all other world religions. Enjoy your journey through *Soul Set Free*, and you too will start calling grace "amazing."

—DOUG CLAY
GENERAL SUPERINTENDENT, GENERAL COUNCIL OF THE
ASSEMBLIES OF GOD

*Soul Set Free* will liberate you from the stuff that is holding you back. Seriously this book will transform your perspective of God and His expectations. John Lindell doesn't try to candy-coat his message—he writes with vulnerability and refreshing honesty. When deciding to read a book, I ask, "Does the author have something to say, or is he or she just trying to make a quick buck?" These days too many books are motivated by payout and prestige. I know you'll agree—this book is different. It has a divine purpose for you and your life. This one will enter your top 10.

—HAL DONALDSON
PRESIDENT AND FOUNDER, CONVOY OF HOPE

This book will help you see God, His grace, and your future in a whole new light! The message of *Soul Set Free* is something every person needs to hear! It comes from the heart of a pastor who is deeply committed to unpacking the truth of God's Word. The pages in this book will move you toward the amazing life God has for you. Highly recommended!

—ROB KETTERLING
LEAD PASTOR, RIVER VALLEY CHURCH

Pastor John is an incredible pastor, leader, family man, and friend. He has accomplished great things in life, one being his passion and mission to present the gospel in such a gracious, profound way. His teaching invites you to eagerly lean in to learn, while challenging and growing you in your personal journey with God. The words written throughout the pages of *Soul Set Free* are life changing. Finding freedom within one's soul is the greatest gift a person could ever receive. This book is going on our must-have list. When a person's soul finds freedom, they are unstoppable.

—ROBERT AND TAYLOR MADU

John Lindell is someone who I believe is able to write about this subject—grace—like few others I know. Grace is something that he has taught, lived, and helped many others experience for themselves throughout his many years of ministry. I completely recommend this book because I believe in the man who wrote it and I know he has lived what he now has written about.

—DINO RIZZO
COFOUNDER AND EXECUTIVE DIRECTOR, ASSOCIATION OF
RELATED CHURCHES (ARC)

Too many followers of Jesus are foolishly trying to graduate from the gospel. Like the Galatians, we start in the Spirit but somehow think we are made perfect by works. In this book the kind, humble, and life-giving leader, pastor, and friend John Lindell sets a course for hope and joy fully fixed in the good news of Jesus Christ. I started living with more freedom after reading the introduction! I can't wait to see what happens in the life of every reader. Prepare to have your soul set free!

—EARL MCCLELLAN
SENIOR PASTOR, SHORELINE CITY CHURCH, DALLAS, TEXAS

Is there news more marvelous than grace? In these pages Pastor John Lindell preaches with bold clarity the message at the heart of Jesus' life, death, and resurrection: that we do have a future, that our lives can be transformed, that the world can be changed—all because we are loved beyond limit by the God who made all there is. Come along with Pastor John to encounter this startling love. You won't be sorry.

—JOSH HAWLEY
US SENATOR

John Lindell's *Soul Set Free* is a personal and unexpected journey into the thoughts of my friend and pastor who I've known for over thirty-five years. If we don't understand grace, we can't fully understand God's commitment to our salvation. The timing of this book is an instruction for today but also reveals how grace frees us from the stigmas and legalism many grow up with. "Grace says you get to be free."

—DOUG PITT
PHILANTHROPIST AND BUSINESSMAN

In his brand-new book John lays out the most practical and insightful revelation about God's grace that I have ever read. John's understanding of God's heart toward us and the way he explains grace are sure to bring lasting soul liberation to everyone who reads this book!

—NANCY ALCORN
FOUNDER AND PRESIDENT, MERCY MULTIPLIED

*Soul Set Free* is a book all Christians should read—from the new believer to the one who has walked with God for decades. Pastor John does a masterful job of exploring the extravagant gift of God's grace. He helps the reader understand grace isn't something to be earned but to be enjoyed. That's a message everyone needs to hear!

—KRISTEN FEOLA
AUTHOR, *THE ULTIMATE GUIDE TO THE DANIEL FAST*

I have come to experience Pastor Lindell—I have seen him be a man of faith, prayer, and commitment to the gospel. Engage this word, and be enthralled by God's work of grace through the might of the gospel for every area of your life.

—ERIC MASON
LEAD PASTOR, EPIPHANY FELLOWSHIP

# SOUL SET FREE

## JOHN LINDELL

CHARISMA
HOUSE

Soul Set Free by John Lindell
Published by Charisma House
Charisma Media/Charisma House Book Group
600 Rinehart Road
Lake Mary, Florida 32746
www.charismahouse.com

Visit the author's website at jamesriver.org, soulsetfreebook.com.

Library of Congress Cataloging-in-Publication Data

Names: Lindell, John, author.
Title: Soul set free / John Lindell.
Description: Lake Mary, Florida : Charisma House, 2019. | Includes bibliographical references and index.
Identifiers: LCCN 2019000197 (print) | LCCN 2019016434 (ebook) | ISBN 9781629996189 (e-book) | ISBN 9781629996172 (hardcover : alk. paper)
Subjects: LCSH: Grace (Theology) | Bible. New Testament Romans--Criticism, interpretation, etc.
Classification: LCC BT761.3 (ebook) | LCC BT761.3 .L56 2019 (print) | DDC 234--dc23
LC record available at https://lccn.loc.gov/2019000197
International Standard Book Number: 978-1-62999-617-2
E-book ISBN: 978-1-62999-618-9

19 20 21 22 23 — 6 5 4 3 2
Printed in the United States of America

To the people of
James River Church

"I thank my God through
Jesus Christ for
all of you."

—ROMANS 1:8, NLT

# CONTENTS

# FOREWORD

I N 2017 Pastor John Lindell extended me the great honor of an invitation to preach at James River Church. I accepted eagerly! You see, James River is alive—one of those infectiously joyful places full of the power of the Spirit. It's been a humbling privilege to partner with the Lindells and their incredible team in a number of capacities since, and when I found out Pastor John was (finally!) writing a book, I was thrilled! And I'm even more delighted that *Soul Set Free* has made its way into your hands.

Before the start of my message that summer morning, Pastor John challenged those gathered at James River to commit to twenty-one days of church-wide fasting and prayer. Naturally when I took the stage, I joked that Pastor John might be just a shirt on a hanger by the end of the fast! If you haven't seen Pastor John, that joke will be lost. Those who have will appreciate the jest. While I know the season of fasting was targeting a spiritual benefit more than physical fitness, let's face it, Pastor John is as in shape as anyone you'll meet!

What's more impressive is Pastor John's spiritual fitness. His life is full of overwhelmingly evident fruits of a long and rich walk with Jesus, one that's fueled by disciplined study, devotion to Scripture, and a hunger to see God glorified. Those who sit under his teaching will agree that his discipline and devotion make him an incredible pastor and shepherd.

I think we tend to look at people like Pastor John—people who have consistently "done the work" of building a rich and thriving relationship with Jesus—and think the visible successes of their lives are the result of their efforts. But I know Pastor John would be the first to say that the work *has already been done* for him, accomplished solely by the miracle power of God's grace. Without grace he'd be up a creek of anxious and exhausted self-reliance, where so many of us are living.

That's what makes me excited about the resource you're holding. You see, it's easy for us to label certain people as grace needy. We create a "grace spectrum" of sorts, putting addicts and those who have wronged us on one end; we see them as obviously in major need of grace! Maybe you picked this book up because you (or someone you're close to) are in that place. Or maybe you're on the opposite end of the spectrum, where we tend to put pastors, church leaders, and "mature" believers. We might even think they've outgrown their need for grace. We forget that grace is our daily bread and by it we breathe our daily breath.

Whether you recognize your desperate hunger for grace or not, I'm so glad you've found this book. It has the potential to change everything about you!

In these pages Pastor John will expertly navigate you through the Book of Romans, Scripture's great grace manifesto. This journey is one we all need to take—it's the way to freedom!

Grace is the key that unlocks true joy and delight in God. It's the gift of all gifts that sets us free from a life of rule keeping, ushering us into the powerful promise of the empty tomb. Ultimately our newfound discovery of His grace will make us fall to our faces in adoration of Him, offering our lives to Him as the only option befitting of those who, by no merit of their own, have had every sin forgiven and every provision made. Grace brought heaven to us since we could never climb there on our own. Grace is God's initiation, beginning to end. It's the invitation that will rearrange our entire grid for living the moment we put our trust in Jesus.

We have a Savior who's ready to drown us in this grace, covering every shortcoming and striving with His perfection. This same Savior promises to lift us, grace drenched, up to true, abundant life. What greater freedom is there than knowing neither our salvation nor our lives depend on our efforts—they are God's creation and His working from beginning to end. By grace God is carrying your life to the good end that He's laid out for you.

I pray this resource makes you hungrier for and more dependent on grace than ever before. I know these pages hold the potential to refresh your view of Jesus and rekindle your love for God. Let them! As you fully recognize what His grace means for you, I believe you'll experience a deep level of meaning and purpose. After all, we can't know who we are until we recognize who God is. This resource will help you greatly to that end. Delight in it!

By grace,
Louie Giglio
Pastor, Passion City Church
Founder, Passion Conferences

# INTRODUCTION

ALL MY LIFE I've heard that the gospel is the good news. And as a working definition, that's fair enough. *Gospel* was originally conceived as a play on words in a time when the Roman Empire proclaimed "the gospel of Caesar," the good news that Caesar's rule was going to usher in peace and prosperity. The apostle Paul uses the word subversively, to say the *really good news* is the news about the life, death, and resurrection of Jesus. But after spending all my adult life as a pastor, I've come to believe that the "good news," as conceived by most Christians, really isn't good news at all. It's *OK* news. It's *fine* news.

I just can't believe that is what God had in mind—for Jesus to come and live and die for us to have the pretty good news, or, at best, the better-than-average news. In reality the news about what Jesus Christ did for us, and what He is in fact still doing, is the *best news* the world has ever heard. The gospel is the key that will unlock your soul and set you free; it's the key that unlocks God's power in every single area of your life. It changes everyone and everything it touches. I want to tell you what I've learned about this best news and how it is revolutionizing my life, even now.

I don't know where you are, or how you are, as you read this. I know the world feels like a volatile and unstable place right now, no matter where you come from or how you see the world. I know the road is hard on many of us, and the

1

toll can get heavy. If you are collapsing under the weight of sorrow and your heart feels fragile for whatever reason—if you can't imagine swinging your legs over the side of the bed and rising to face the storm one more day—I have certainly written this book with you in mind.

But just as much so, I've written this book for people who are not necessarily in the midst of some existential crisis, not necessarily on the verge of total collapse. Of course we all get to those dire, difficult moments, where the journey feels relentless. But I am writing just as much to those of you who don't feel the road you've been traveling is especially exhilarating, nor is it so brutal you just can't take it—or maybe right now, the road doesn't *feel like* much of anything. The long miles keep unfolding monotonously, like driving through those parts of the Midwest when one field starts to become indistinguishable from the rest, or through Highway 50 in Nevada, the so-called "loneliest road in America," which is almost all desert.

Maybe you've kept the car maintained just well enough to keep you going, the wheels still turning—and you keep moving on, regardless of what happens. You aren't thriving, and may not even be giving much thought to whether or not you are thriving…you're just surviving. Cruising. You get lost in the highway stare, not too reflective on where you are, where you've come from, or where you are headed, because it takes all that you've got to just keep yourself on the road and between the lines. It's not awful. There may not feel like much to complain about in the grand scheme of things. Life just…is. It may not feel quite melancholy per se, just mundane.

Or maybe you are more like me. I was never bored with

my life. I saw the Christian life as a race, and I was in it to win it. For me it was about grit, determination, hard work, following through, and keeping my word! I did everything I knew to do to live in a way that was obedient and faithful. But no matter how hard or fast I ran, I still felt something was missing.

I was acutely aware of this when I saw people around me living the Christian life with a kind of joy and ease that seemed to elude me. How was it that I did not have that same sense of delight, that freshness to my faith, when I was putting in so much effort? Shouldn't there be at least some sense of exhilaration, passion, joy…power? There may not be any one particular thing keeping you awake at night, just a growing, nagging feeling—as I had—that *there must surely be more than this.*

If you are in such a place right now, passing that I-know-I'm-missing-something-but-I-don't-know-what-it-is mile marker, this book is especially for you. Because I'm convinced that the God who spoke worlds into existence, called all created things into being, and then sent Jesus into a fallen, fractured world to win back His sons and daughters, did not intend for your life to be "just fine." Nor did He intend for you to be utterly exhausted from trying to live a life of faith from your own effort.

I can't imagine that God would go to such lengths to draw us to Himself as beloved sons and daughters if He didn't have a plan for something richer, deeper, and fuller. God spared no expense on His kids. He went all out to lavish His love upon us. I'm not talking about a fairy tale where money falls out of the sky and every stray whim is gratified; I'm talking about living with power, clarity, and purpose.

I believe that kind of life is not only attainable but is also possible right here, right now, at this very moment. You don't have to die to have it. You don't have to change jobs or upgrade your house, your spouse, or your kids to have it. There is power available to you that can unlock your soul and all of its hidden longings—the buried hopes of the past, the strength needed for the moment, and the dreams for a beautiful future. That is the power of the best news: the gospel is able to change your life at this moment, even now.

## THE ONE WORD THAT CHANGES EVERYTHING

What is this power that can close the distance between just fine, pretty good, and the best? What is this key that can unlock your very soul? It's all bound up in a single word—*grace*.

If you've had even casual encounters with the church, then *grace* is a word you know all too well. We sing about it in our most universally beloved hymn: "Amazing grace! How sweet the sound that saved a wretch like me!"[1] When people bow their heads to pray before a meal to give thanks, we sometimes call this saying grace. If we see a person moving with a sort of ease and beauty, a man or woman fully at home in his or her skin, the kind of person who lights up a room—we might say they are graceful. If a friend unexpectedly takes you out to dinner, you would call him gracious. It's a word we think we know.

Grace is the mystery at the bottom of all the others. It is the most distinguishing feature of the gospel, what sets Christianity apart from every other world religion. It's such a simple word to say, and yet it seems as if all the beauty of the gospel is somehow bound up in it. *Grace* is the word that changes everything. Philip Yancey writes, "Grace means there is nothing I can do to make God love me more, and nothing I can do to make God love me less."[2]

Yet I am convinced that most of us don't know exactly what grace is, much less how it works or the difference it can make in our lives. After all my years of serving as senior pastor at James River Church and seeing countless lives changed by God, my experience is this: most Christians struggle to access grace for themselves, no matter how well they might speak about it.

We struggle to believe God could have really loved us in our deepest, darkest moment when we said or did the thing of which we are most ashamed.

We struggle to believe God could love us in the midst of addiction.

We struggle with the idea that grace can truly cover our past, sustain us in the present, and even extend into our future.

We can't fathom that grace is a bottomless, limitless resource that will never run out.

I've seen it over and over again in the eyes of people I have loved and served—and if I'm honest, even in the eyes looking back at me in the mirror. We are all too aware of all our flaws and imperfections. Deep down it's hard to believe God is really that good. It's hard to believe He could really love us that much.

I decided to write this book because I believe God's grace is far bigger, better, and wilder than you could ever imagine. I wrote this for every person who has ever wondered if God's grace is really wide enough, broad enough, deep enough, to erase the shame of your past. I wrote this for every person who has ever wondered if His grace is sufficient for the moment you're in right now and if it will be enough for your future. I wrote this for every person who struggles to comprehend the depth and breadth of His grace, and for every person who struggles to extend grace to the people around them.

This is not a self-help book—making extravagant promises if you follow this diet, try this technique, repeat this mantra. The astonishing thing about grace is that "the work" is really not up to you at all; it is the proclamation that the work has already been done for you and is being done in and through you. "There remains a Sabbath rest for the people of God," the Book of Hebrews says (4:9). And everywhere I go, I meet sons and daughters of God who are exhausted from trying to do all the heavy lifting themselves, trying to earn God's approval, trying to prove they are worthy, trying to outrun their shame or their past.

Grace says everything that ever needed to be done has been done for you already. Grace says you can finally lay the burden down, let the people who hurt you off the hook—even let yourself off the hook. Grace says there's nothing else you have to do to make yourself right or righteous—that the only response God expects from you in response to His radical forgiveness is to come on home where you belong. Grace says you get to start over. Grace says you get to be free.

Grace says there is enough for you, and enough for everyone you care about—that there will always be enough. Grace says you are living in God's abundance, in a world where everyone seems to operate out of a sense of scarcity. Grace says nothing is irreversible, no verdict is final, and there are no dead ends. The best news is that grace is not some hazy thing out in the distance somewhere. His grace is here. His grace is for you. His grace is now, holding you, sustaining you, filling every moment.

You aren't asked to do anything about it—except believe. Put all your weight down on grace and the God who offers it. Accept it. Live in light of it; live as if you can really trust it. You and I have many barriers to letting ourselves be fully convinced of it—some outside of us, but most inside of us. Living as if grace is real, solid, and true can be easier said than done. But if you dare risk to believe it, grace changes everything—most of all, you.

## BROKEN OPEN TO GRACE

I spent some time in Europe studying Martin Luther, who struggled in his relationship with God because of his experience with his father. Luther's father, Hans, was an unrelenting man who had designs for his son to become a lawyer. When Martin dropped out of law school after less than one year to become a monk, his father was furious at what he saw as a waste of his education. But even—and perhaps especially—while living an ordered life of religious devotion, his distance from his father seemed to set the agenda for his entire life: no matter what he did or how well he behaved, Luther felt tormented by his own guilt, unworthiness, and condemnation.

It was precisely this lifelong struggle, though, that prepared Luther to be broken open to a radical message of grace. Luther, like his hero the apostle Paul, was a zealot who minded his manners and kept all the rules. A lot of us hard-working, doing-the-best-we-can types suspect that if things are good between God and us, surely it's because we are trying really hard to keep the rules. And perhaps this is why, from Paul to Luther to a much smaller figure in the church's story like mine, there has to come a moment when life breaks you open.

Ultimately it's about being broken open to love. For me there was a particular moment on an airplane when all that had been stirring underneath finally bubbled up to the surface. The feelings in my heart finally found expression in words. I don't know exactly why it all hit me that day the way it did. Being the kind of person who has always worked hard on my life on the ground, maybe there was something about being thirty thousand feet in the air that finally gave me a different perspective.

I've had a full life in many ways, and there is so much I am grateful for. But I'll never be able to unsee what I saw that day on the plane: that for all the ways I have seen God at work in my life, grace still eluded me. And I knew that somehow, sometime, I had to find it, hold it, grasp it, and know it in a way I had not known it before.

I wonder if you've ever had such a moment, a kind of divine disruption that breaks you open to a grace more ferocious than you ever dreamed. If you haven't, there is no better time than the present. That's the beautiful thing about life with God—you get to start again from wherever you are, no matter how you got there. Make a mental note of where you are sitting as you read these words and prepare to embark on this journey with me. I pray that this precise spot, in this exact moment, would be the start of your own awakening to radical, revolutionary grace.

## Chapter 1

# ON THE ROAD
# TOWARD GRACE

All are justified freely by his grace through
the redemption that came by Christ Jesus.
—ROMANS 3:24, NIV

I was sitting on the plane next to my wife, Debbie, on our way to Florida for a much-needed rest when I felt a peculiar churning in my stomach. The clouds had been gathering for a while—not quite a storm, just that growing, nagging sense that something wasn't quite right. I hadn't been able to put my finger on it.

In a month both Debbie and I would celebrate our fiftieth birthdays. I was conscious that nearing our fifties, in many ways we were in one of the best seasons of our life together. We're still as in love as ever. We have three grown, healthy, beautiful children we adore and a whole flock of grandchildren. Our home is filled with love and laughter. We are surrounded by community, too—throughout twenty-five years pastoring James River Church in Springfield, Missouri, we've seen a dynamic move of God that has resulted in fifteen thousand gathering for worship every week.

I know I'm a blessed man, rich in all the treasures you cannot buy, and I take none of it for granted. Life is good, the ministry is good—I'm doing work that gives me a strong sense of purpose, meaning, and a feeling that I've been able to serve something that is changing the world in some small way. In full disclosure, I don't consider myself an especially reflective person. I inherited my dad's strong work ethic, and I've done the best I can with what I've been given. I try to be present for what God has called me to do, keep my head to the ground, and not try to take my own emotional temperature every few minutes. But I couldn't deny it anymore that day on the plane—*something just wasn't right.*

With time above the clouds for my mind to wander, I finally broke the silence and told Debbie, "You know, I'm a messed-up dude."

"Why is that?" she asked.

Point of fact, I value stability and security and live a fairly tightly ordered life. I am not known as a messed-up dude, generally, even to those closest to me. I'm more methodical, grounded, and to the best of my ability, in control. But in this unguarded moment it all came tumbling out: I'm a preacher. I love Jesus. I've loved Jesus all my adult life. I've preached Jesus and seen hundreds if not thousands of people place their faith in Him. I've seen the difference He makes in people's real lives. I've always believed what I preach and lived it to the best of my ability.

There was just one small problem: I wasn't sure if I actually *loved* God the Father. Not really. Even now it feels odd to articulate in print, just like it did for me to say out loud that day. Given all I've seen and experienced, and all the ways God the Father has blessed me and provided for me, how could I not love Him? I had been taught that Jesus would take a bullet for me. So on one level I knew that I did, in fact, love Jesus—and as Christians, we do believe that Jesus is God.

But what about this God that Jesus called Father? That figure, for all I'd heard about Him and read about Him and preached about Him, still felt more obscure, more ambiguous to me. I believed He was good, as a matter of dogma. I had no difficulty respecting Him, reverencing Him, or even worshipping Him. I wanted to love Him, but I wasn't sure that I did. And I certainly didn't feel like He could really love me.

There are many things you can respect or react to with a sense of awe and wonder but not necessarily love. I respect the ocean—vast, powerful, endless, beautiful. It inspires a sense of reverence in me. But how precisely does one love something as vast and wild and boundaryless as the ocean? God the Father was still like that for me. It was easy for me to bow a knee to Him, sing to Him, and thank Him for my food. But the gap I felt growing inside of me was a sense of distance. It was *polite* distance, but distance nonetheless.

It made me think of John Wesley writing to his brother Charles in his mid-sixties, after already seeing the Methodist revival God ignited in and through him sweep the globe. In a moment of personal introspection he realized his love for God was less than it should have been. He wrote, "I do not love God. I never did," even though he saw countless souls come to saving faith through his proclamation of that God. He wanted "all the world to come" to what he himself in that moment did not feel.[1]

Many Christians have been there; maybe you are there right now. Like Wesley, it's not that you aren't a Christian, but you realize there is something missing in your love for God. You may love God in general, and you may love Jesus, but do you love the Father? Do you feel a personal connection to Him and understand just how much He loves you? Questions similar to those were stirring deep inside my heart; it was almost as if a hole had been slowly opening in me.

Reflecting on all of this, I told Debbie on the plane that day, "I just don't feel like I really get it. I just don't. I don't *get* grace." I need to get it. I'm a pastor—I'm supposed to get it! But in my heart I knew it was true: the grace that animates every movement in the symphony of Scripture, the grace that burned hot like fire in the apostle Paul, the grace I have heard myself preach in countless sermons still somehow seemed just out of my grasp.

It wasn't that I didn't know "about" it. I knew all about it, in a way. On an intellectual level grace had always been present in my life. I'm a logical man and a verse-by-verse Bible teacher. I knew grace as a concept, a construct, a theory, a doctrine. I believed in grace because I've watched it sweep through people's lives, turning chaos into beauty. I've witnessed it firsthand in our church over and over.

Since I preached grace conceptually, maybe in one way I preached ahead of my experience. But there's also a very real way that you can only genuinely preach what you know. And on some level grace was not something I quite yet knew. There was this part of me that felt like an outsider to it, as if I was pressing my face up against the glass looking in, observing, longing.

I've wondered if some people, by virtue of temperament or experience, just get a hold of grace easier than the rest of us. My wife, Debbie, is one of those people—she grasps grace intuitively. She has an ease with herself and others, a joy, a playfulness that just oozes grace. Enjoying her walk with God never seemed hard for her like it was for me. For me it was always a matter of hard work and discipline. For her it seemed doing life with God was less structured, more relational, and a whole lot more relaxed. We both read the same Bible. We theoretically know the same God. But in some way that I could never quite get my hands around, it just seemed like she was having more fun than I was, and I didn't know why.

I am very much my father's son. All my life I've been driven and competitive. I'm the sort of person who thinks doing more than what is required is good, and doing too much is just about right.

## ELDER BROTHER SYNDROME

In Luke's Gospel, Jesus tells a story about a prodigal son. At least that is how people know of the story—in reality it isn't just the story of a prodigal son; it's actually the story of two lost sons. One has stayed home his entire life, the elder son in a culture in which being the firstborn meant everything. He had kept the rules, been honorable and respectable like his father, been an exemplary son. His younger brother, on the other hand, did an unspeakable thing: he asked for his inheritance early so he could leave home and spend it however he wanted. It was an insulting request, surely belittling to a man of dignity—the cultural equivalent of saying, "I wish you were dead."

The son went out and spent his inheritance the way any young man would—on all the toys and pleasure he could get into. Before long he'd squandered all of it and ultimately had to take a job working in a hog pen—the vilest, filthiest profession imaginable for the product of an orthodox Jewish home. It was while feeding the scraps to these animals, deemed ceremonially unclean by his culture, that a revelation came on the tail end of another hunger pang: even the servants at my father's house have it better than this. At that moment "he came to himself" (Luke 15:17)—he remembered who he was, who his father was, and who he was called to be. This is surely how any journey with God must start—some vague memory of home, a remembering of who we are as sons and daughters created in the image of God.

The realization settled on him like morning dew, and he immediately started plotting and scheming. The best he could imagine, from the low place, was that his father might be interested in striking up some kind of a business arrangement, letting him come back to the farm as a kind of indentured servant. A fast talker and a charmer by nature, he started rehearsing the speech in his head, hoping against all the odds that his dad might be open to it. Covered in filth, he left the pigs and started on the long journey home, replaying his little speech over and over again, hoping to say it just right, with the right inflection...hoping he would seem sorry enough, broken enough. He felt the knot in his stomach, though, when he was within sight of the village—hunger now overridden by anxiety. He braced himself for the worst.

---

This is surely how any journey with God must start—some vague memory of home, a remembering of who we are as sons and daughters created in the image of God.

---

And then the truly shocking thing happened: before the son could even get to the house, he saw a dot in the distance come bolting toward him. It was jarring at first. He had left the village in a patriarchal culture in the rudest, most disgraceful way imaginable. Was somebody already running out to tell him he had no business coming back here? As the blur of color in the robe got close and features became visible, he wiped his eyes—surely he had seen a ghost. It looked like his father; it was his unmistakable gait. But it seemed impossible, as wealthy, respectable, land-owing fathers in the ancient Middle East didn't run anywhere for any reason; it was considered beneath their standing. But it was him—it was really him!

As the son took a deep breath, already struggling to hang on to the trail of words evaporating from his mind, his father tackled him. They were on the ground, covered in dirt like children, the old man laughing hysterically, the son wet from the tears running down his father's beard. He couldn't get a word in for his father covering him with kisses. "My son, my son!" He was crying and laughing, laughing and crying, utterly oblivious to the crowd of servants and villagers gathering to watch the spectacle. "Quick! Get me my ring, my robe, and my sandals—I'm giving them to my boy to wear. Kill the fattest cow we've got. Invite all the neighbors. My boy—*my boy*—my boy is home!"

From the edge of the porch the boy's elder brother watched the scene unfold—his father throwing his dignity out the window in front of the community—and quietly seethed. "I've been here all these years, kept the rules, minded my manners and my father's affairs, and nobody ever threw me a party!" A polite, well-behaved young man's decades' worth of simmering rage boiled to the surface.

When it came time for the party—an event the elder son would have been culturally obligated to host on his father's behalf—he couldn't bring himself to greet the kid. His father came to check on him. "What's wrong, son?"

Finally he unleashed all of it: "I just don't get it, Dad! How can you treat him like this? What has he ever done for you? I've done everything I've been asked to do, without fail. But there was no party for me, no dancing or drinks. But he goes out and spends your hard-earned money on whores, and this is what he gets?" His chest and neck were splotched bright red, every word spat out with fire.

But no anger darkened the face of his father. His eyes

were wide and tender as he walked over and placed a hand on each of his son's shoulders. "My son." He paused until his firstborn son finally looked him in the eye. "Don't you know that all I have is yours? That you could have any of this, anytime that you wanted? Don't you see—it was as if your brother was dead, and now he's come back to life! How can we not celebrate? Please, won't you come and join the party?"

Hopefully now you see that it's not really a story about the prodigal. There are *two* lost sons, and the story is about the distance between each of them and their father. One—the wild, impertinent, burn-it-all-down son—bridges the space between them, comes back home, and falls into his father's embrace. The other son has been on his father's porch all along, but there's more space between him and his dad than his prodigal brother had experienced from hundreds of miles away. Geographically he was right there. But his heart could not have been further.

The weight of the story lands not on the prodigal, who is already home, welcomed, and delighted in, but the lingering question of the elder son. What will he do? Grace makes its way easily to those who need it most, to those who live fast and hard, speeding their lives into the wall early on.

But what about the quieter, more respectable older sons and daughters—those of us who have always harbored some deep suspicion that to whatever extent God does love, like, or approve of us, it is because we have done our part *or at least tried really hard to get it right*. Elder sons like me may have never really had reason to feel our distance from the father the way the prodigal does through his more colorful, visceral journey.

But that doesn't mean the distance is not there. In fact, the end of the story shows that while the prodigal is celebrating at home, the elder son has never been further away. Often for elder sons and daughters it's not until some random moment on an airplane or some stray hard feelings toward the prodigal arise that we realize how far we are from home.

## HOW GRACE CHANGES EVERYTHING

My life wasn't changed on the plane, but the journey to go deeper into grace was instantly accelerated. There is something liberating about giving voice to your questions and coming to terms with your deficiencies. The conversation stayed with me, and in the weeks that followed I increasingly realized that my understanding of God as a Father, better yet as *my* Father, needed some work. I began to study God the Father, paying close attention to His love for people and personalizing His love for me. The more I read and meditated on His love, the more real it became to me.

As the months passed, it became increasingly clear that grace is the framework by which the love of the Father is explored and expressed. When you've spent all of your adult life preaching to people every week, it's humbling to see that it's taken so long to grasp the revelation of grace for yourself. I've had to acknowledge that sometimes I don't think I have been very *gracious* because I've not fully known *grace*. But since that day when I finally came to terms with my own bankrupt understanding of grace, I've slowly been coming to *see*. That's what grace does—it heals your eyes, and nothing looks the same. You are able to view Scripture, the world around you, and perhaps most of all your own self through healed eyes. Grace is a whole different way of seeing the world.

As my heart was opened to this newfound desperation to grasp His ungraspable grace, I stumbled into the Book of

Romans again. Romans is the apostle Paul's greatest work, his magnum opus. For Christians, it is the Magna Carta of grace!

Seventeen hundred years ago, when a young Augustine was outside with his friend in Milan, he heard the voice of a child singing a song: "Pick it up, read it; pick it up, read it." He thought it was related to a children's game at first, but he could not recall ever hearing those words before. Sensing there was something divine about this encounter, he picked up a Bible, opened it, and read the first passage he saw— from the Book of Romans. He was never the same.[2]

It was also the Book of Romans that initiated Martin Luther's awakening twelve hundred years later and sowed the seeds of a grace reformation in him. Hearing Luther's preface to Romans read aloud stirred yet another revolution in John Wesley, who felt his heart "strangely warmed" just hearing Luther's testimony of how Romans had changed him.[3]

I'm a low-drama kind of guy, and my story is subtler than these. I make no claims of being an Augustine, Luther, or Wesley. But in my own way I felt it was the Spirit that somehow led me back to this primal grace text after years of pastoring. And as I preached through Romans, I realized this story of amazing grace really had become my own story—the story I had been slowly living my way into all along, and the story I most wanted to tell the world.

Because I love Scripture and tend to keep the emphasis on Scripture when I preach, many people in our church haven't heard me tell my own story of how all this came to live in me. As much as I want to be vulnerable, I generally enjoy telling people Bible stories more than I do telling my own story. But it feels urgent to share it with you in the pages of this book. First, because I think it could be the key to unlocking your own story, and second, because I know from firsthand experience that it actually works. I want you to come to understand the grace of God in a way that it was never explained to me.

When I dove again into Paul's magnificent letter with my defenses down and my heart cracked wide open, I saw colors there I could not see before. Suddenly the good news was *really* good news, and it was actually changing my life! For the first time I began to catch a glimpse of the way He sees me. I started to see what it means for Him to choose me, *for Him to pick me.*

I started to see how unsurprised He was by my failures and how relentlessly committed He was to seeing this process all the way through to complete transformation. I finally started to see that when I fell down, there was no need to start again as if nothing that came before counted. That is just not how God works.

I take my role as a father very seriously, and I love my children more than just about anything. As I worked my way through Romans again, I began to see that there is no way I could be more loving to my own children than God is to me. If they come to me with a struggle, I intuitively know they need more of me, not less. How could God be any different? I could feel the truth of grace starting to shift my insides; I could feel my own soul giving way to this radical freedom.

How do I know that when you truly grasp God's amazing grace, it will change your life? Because it has changed mine. And it is still changing me, even now.

## Chapter 2

# THERE IS GRACE FOR YOU

Paul, a servant of Christ Jesus, called to be an apostle, set apart for the gospel of God...

—ROMANS 1:1

**W**E NEVER REALLY know where the road is going to lead, especially if God is on it with us. There are all sorts of bends and surprises. During a sabbatical a few years ago I spent a week white water rafting the Grand Canyon. We rafted a few miles and were setting up camp for the first time at a beach on the canyon floor. It seemed red ants were everywhere. When the guide began his orientation, he told us the ants would leave us alone if we left them alone, but if we swatted them, we would get bit. As some of the campers began grabbing tents, he added, "If I were you, I'd skip the tent. It's ninety degrees down here; a tent will only make it fifteen degrees hotter when you try to sleep."

He continued: "We'll give you a bucket for your simple business because you don't want to go down by the toilets at night—there are pink rattlesnakes around. And of course, the wolf spiders. If one of those bites you, we'll have to get you airlifted out by chopper to the nearest hospital."

Then he told us, "Also be careful not to shake out your blanket in the morning after you sleep because you could have scorpions inside. And if one of them happens to crawl on you during the night, don't swat at it—you don't want to get stung. So just let them crawl on."

Seriously? There wasn't anything written in the travel brochures about pink rattlesnakes and wolf spiders. I glanced at my friend and then smiled as I watched some of our fellow rafters. Suffice it to say, every trip has unexpected surprises!

That was certainly true for Saul, the man who would go on to write the Book of Romans, which is still the ultimate field guide to grace even now, two thousand years after it was written. He seemed to be the least likely person to get the grace message. So before we travel with him down that

Romans road that leads to grace, we must first understand something of the man who wrote it—the fiery, passionate, enigmatic apostle Paul. There is no rowdier or more polarizing figure in the New Testament than the former Saul of Tarsus.

As Paul will note himself, his critics said he wasn't impressive in person. One early ancient source describes him as "a man of small stature, with a bald head and crooked legs...with eye-brows meeting and nose somewhat hooked."[1] But even if his looks didn't knock people out, his words are still knocking us out to this day. Paul was a fierce, brilliant intellectual—but not an ivory tower sort of brainiac. His unique genius was the product of both a rough-and-tumble life and, ultimately, an even more rough-and-tumble encounter with God.

Paul was, in his own words, "a Jew of Jews." (In general, he was the sort of guy who, if you want to know all the things that were terrific about him, would happily tell you himself!) He had the right bloodline, the right pedigree, and a white-hot zeal for God. Young Saul knew the Torah (the Hebrew Law) better than the dusty backroads of his hometown of Tarsus and devoted his whole life to keeping it. Even as a young man he was an expert in the Law. And because he felt like he mastered the Law, he knew who was in and who was out; who was doing it right and who was doing it wrong.

When young Saul started hearing rumors about a new Jewish cult that claimed the murdered Jesus of Nazareth had somehow risen from the dead and was the long-expected Jewish Messiah—the Anointed or Chosen One who would redeem Israel—it raised his ire. "These people are heretics," Paul thought. "Somebody should do something!" There was no way this Jesus could be the Messiah. He bucked too much of the priestly purity code, as did His disciples. And Saul, a serious Jew not given to idle talk, wives' tales, or idle speculation, would hear nothing of this resurrection business. There was too much at stake to let these rabble-rousers stir up his fellow Jews, working them into a frenzy with their fairy tales of resurrection.

Saul was so sure of his convictions that when a group of his colleagues decided to make an example out of one of those early grace rebels, a man named Stephen, he happily rode along with them and watched over their coats. He nodded in approval as the men pounded Stephen with rocks, one after another—*Thwack! Thwack! Thwack!*—the stones breaking skin and shattering bone until Stephen bled to death in front of them. A haunting grin covered Stephen's face as he looked into the sky with bright eyes at the very last. It was an image Saul couldn't quite shake loose, no matter how much he wanted to.

In contemporary vernacular Saul was a religious terrorist. But in his mind at the time he was just a really devout Jew who was willing to toe the line at all costs. Then one day he was going down a familiar road he'd traveled hundreds of times before—the road to Damascus—when a crazy thing happened: a blinding light shone on him. *Blinding* is not a metaphor here for really bright—it literally blinded him!

Saul just stood there, sightless, his heart racing in terror. Then he heard a voice call his name. "Saul, Saul," the voice said, "Why are you persecuting Me?" He looked toward where the sound came from but couldn't see anything; looked toward his companions but couldn't see them either. It was like the voice was all around and in him—like it filled everything in them.

With a tremble in his voice, he asked, "Who are You?"

And the voice that came out of the light introduced Himself: "I'm Jesus. You know—the one you are persecuting."

Right there on the spot Jesus the Christ told Saul the killer of Christians that He had a job for him, that He was putting him to work, and that he'd see and suffer much on account of His name. Everything he did for the rest of his life could be traced back to that moment. Frederick Buechner wrote about it in *Peculiar Treasures*.

> Everything he ever said or wrote or did from that day forward was an attempt to bowl over the human race as he'd been bowled over himself while he lay there with dust in his mouth and road apples down the front of his shirt: *Don't fight them, join them. He wants you on his side.* YOU, of all people. ME. Who in the world, who in the solar system, the galaxy, could ever have expected it?[2]

Saul staggered away from this encounter blind until he was led to the house of a man named Ananias who, like all the early Christians, was scared to death of Saul the murderer. But the voice that spoke to Saul spoke to Ananias, too, and told him to receive this violent enemy.

Ananias greeted him—not with swear words, but with a simple, beautiful greeting: "Brother Saul!" And the moment Saul was accepted and called "brother," the scales fell off his eyes and he was able to see. He was blinded as Saul, but he opened his eyes as Paul—a whole new set of eyes, a whole new way of seeing the world.

"I once was lost, but now am found; was blind, but now I see," the hymn tells us.[3] This is what the gospel has always been about—like the blind man in John 9, those that could not see are suddenly seeing clearly. The folks who think they see clearly, like the Pharisees in Jesus' time or Saul before he ran smack-dab into Jesus on the road to Damascus, actually don't see anything at all. Grace, for Paul and for us, is a way of seeing.

Grace is what we see after we see the light. After Paul encountered Jesus, he staggered away from that encounter—not under the blinding light anymore but nonetheless drunk on God. His experience of Jesus was so bright, so mesmerizing, so stunning, that it changed his name and the entire trajectory of his life. The man who had been passionate about killing Christians was now even more passionate about the Christ who accosted him on the road to Damascus.

The man once feared as the enemy of the church would now be seen as the enemy of the state, threatening Caesar and the Roman Empire with a radical gospel of grace. In a time when the message "Caesar is lord" was written on every coin and building, Paul went around telling people "Jesus is Lord." People called him a traitor, but the church called him an apostle. Because his strange encounter with Jesus changed his life forever, he in turn changed the world as we know it.

> We are all unlikely candidates for grace. It has been that way from the beginning.

The man who had been a terrorist to the early church became a terror to the powers of darkness. The very God he had been persecuting was not angry with him; He didn't come down to smite him, but to save him. Paul found out firsthand that Love can grab you by the collar, turn you inside out, throw you to the ground, pick you up, and give you a brand-new name. He found out that no one is past saving and no past is beyond redeeming. There are no dead ends, and that is very, very good news.

For one reason or another you may not feel you are the most likely candidate for grace. But that's OK—we are all unlikely candidates for grace. It has been that way from the beginning.

## FROM THE DAMASCUS ROAD
## TO THE ROMANS ROAD

Paul's life was so captured by the light on the Road to Damascus that he devoted his life to sharing it with others. Grace changed his entire trajectory. By the time he wrote the Book of Romans, Paul had been traveling provinces bordering the Aegean Sea for about ten years, and he had finally set his sights on going to Rome. Before he left, he sat down to write a letter to the believers there.

It appears there were several Christian communities in Rome, all of them almost certainly small and meeting in houses. These churches, like our churches now, were complicated and full of conflicts—in their case, often between Jewish believers, whose lives were still largely oriented around the synagogue, and Gentile (non-Jewish) Christians, who had come to believe in Jesus as Messiah (or Anointed One) outside the temple establishment. They weren't any less troubled than any of our churches are, even though the apostles preached in them.

By the time Paul sat down to write to this small cluster

of house churches in Rome in advance of his visit, he had known every conceivable kind of pain. Paul had lived long enough to have scars that told some stories. He knew what it was to be guilty, to be the accused. He knew what it was to be beaten, hated, despised, rejected. He knew what it was to have the people he loved and served turn on him and betray him. He had more than his own share of dark nights.

But as Paul prepared to head to Rome, having no idea what the city or the emperor had in store for him, his mind surely flickered back to the road to Damascus. He remembered what it was like before he heard the voice. He remembered both the terror and the tenderness of the encounter. He remembered the power of this gospel—what it did to him and how it changed him.

The gospel, when he heard it, opened up new possibilities for him. We often refer to the Damascus Road as Paul's conversion, but keep in mind that when he arrived at Ananias' house, he was still blind—stumbling toward the truth, yes; feeling his way toward it. But he could not yet see.

What changed everything, ultimately, was how God saw him! God sees us not just as we are, but as we can (and through the power of the gospel, must) yet become. And it happened for Paul the way it happens for so many of us— someone utters a word over us that doesn't speak to who or where we've been, but to where we can go. Ananias called him brother. He spoke a word of friendship over him while he was yet considered an enemy.

## TRANSFORMATION FROM
## THE INSIDE OUT

Maybe you, like Paul, have a hard time seeing yourself as a likely candidate for this kind of transformation. I wasn't the most likely person for this kind of life, either. My sweet mother once told somebody she had secretly feared I'd wind up in prison! Looking back, I can see why. Growing up, I spent a lot of school time standing in the corner, sitting in the hall, or serving detention. Had the trajectory of my life not been interrupted by God's grace, things could have gotten ugly.

More recently my mother came across one of our services at James River on GodTV and told me it made her cry. She said, "In that moment I was overwhelmed that *you* had become a preacher." It's safe to say that the last thing she expected was for her son to become a preacher! In the same way, Saul's companions on the road to Damascus never expected the man who murdered Christians to spend the rest of his life spreading the name of Jesus, the name he had worked so hard to make people forget.

But then the moment comes when grace just gets a hold of you.

When grace got a hold of Saul, the rest of his journey was not like the first stage—when it was all about gritting his teeth, keeping the rules, obeying the Law at all costs for the sake of the Law. In the second stage of his journey, he didn't do the same things.

When grace gets ahold of a person and that person gets a hold of grace, amazing things happen. Just like Saul got a new name, when I grasped the grace of God and His incredible love for me, things began to change—not because

I was suddenly preoccupied with keeping rules, but because love began to well up in me as a natural response to the grace I received. Instead of keeping rules or trying to gain favor, I experienced a fresh joy in knowing that I was already accepted and that God was at work in me.

The way this kind of transformation occurs, though, is never from outside to inside. We don't change our behavior and then change our hearts. Rather, God speaks to us in such a way that changes our hearts, and that change slowly starts to inform our actions. That's the astonishing thing about how God works—He speaks His words of love and friendship over us "while we were still sinners," in the words of Romans 5:8.

In the beginning nothing about us has changed. We just gradually start to believe what God has already said about us. God's unconditional love comes to us at our worst, and we get the first taste of God's *best*—and it's a taste we can never get over.

## THERE IS GRACE

There is much more in the pages ahead about what grace is, how it works, and how it transforms us. But if you put this book down today and never read another word, the thing I'd most want you to know is this:

- No matter who you are or where you come from; no matter what you've done or how many times you've done it—*there is grace for you.*

- If you are laboring under a constant sense of unworthiness, feeling like you never quite measure up—*there is grace for you.*

- If you struggle with legalism and judgment, always trying to earn God's approval (or someone else's, for that matter)—*there is grace for you.*

- If you struggle to let go of the past, to let go of some hurt that was inflicted on you or to forgive the person who inflicted the damage—*there is grace for you.*

- If you are fighting with an addiction or some habitual, besetting sin—*there is grace for you.*

- If you struggle to get out of your head and into your heart; if you feel that no matter what you might learn about God, you're never quite able to enter into a life of trust and freedom—*there is grace for you.*

There is grace for everybody, and there is grace for everything—if we will open our eyes and our hearts to it!

Some people worry that if we understand grace too well, we may take it as a license to sin. It is true: if grace is taught correctly, it *will* be abused! But my primary motivation isn't to keep you from messing up. We have all felt ourselves live as less than we are called to be. We've all done things we aren't proud of. But in all of that, there is a loving God who keeps moving us forward.

And once you get past the initial scandal of grace—that it really does cover you in all the ways you need to be covered—you will come to see that this grace that covers you also empowers you to change, to grow, even to be formed into the likeness of Christ. Grace doesn't just cover us—grace transforms us. Knowing how much God loves us makes all the difference in the world; it directly impacts the kinds of people we will become.

This is the grace that swept up a ragtag collection of saints and sinners throughout the ages—evidently including pastors who never thought they'd grasp it for themselves. I just had no idea how radically it could revolutionize even an experienced Christian. When you get hold of it—or better yet, when it gets hold of you—you will feel like a prisoner set free. I have finally started to shed the old skin of joyless Christianity that felt nearly impossible to live.

My simple hope and prayer for you, regardless of how you got this book in your hands, is that as you read about grace here, it will make you love God more because you will more fully understand how much God loves you. Paul's closing prayer for the believers at Ephesus was that they "may have strength to comprehend with all the saints what is the breadth and length and height and depth, and to know the love of Christ that surpasses knowledge, that you may be filled with all the fullness of God" (Eph. 3:18–19). That's quite a prayer—to comprehend the incomprehensible, to know the unknowable. But there is a knowing that transcends knowledge, a revelation that surpasses learning. There is a way of seeing not only into the Book of Romans but also into the depths of the heart of God Himself.

That is why I join Paul in making this my prayer: because I know the things you need to see are above my pay grade to show you. But I also know there is a God who delights in you, who hovers over you even now; who desperately longs to show you the unshowable, to open up the eyes of your heart to see that which even angels long to see. Grace is stunning, breathtaking. There is no corner of your heart or life that it will leave untouched. When you understand how loved you are, it changes how you love others; you learn to extend the same grace that is constantly extended to you.

Here's a mild spoiler alert for what's ahead—no matter how much you grasp the beauty of God's love for you in any given minute, there is always more. It never runs out.

## Chapter 3

# THE BEST NEWS YOU'VE NEVER HEARD

I am not ashamed of the gospel, for it is the power of God for salvation to everyone who believes, to the Jew first and also to the Greek. For in it the righteousness of God is revealed from faith for faith, as it is written, "The righteous shall live by faith."

—ROMANS 1:16–17

A T THE HEART of the Book of Romans is one big idea, captured early in the book, that frames all the other big ideas that follow from it. This is the idea that changed Paul's life, took him from Saul to Paul, and turned him inside out and upside down. Romans 1:16–17 (shown above) encapsulates the core message of this massively influential book.

The central vision of this letter and all of Paul's work are two words that animate everything else he does and says: *the gospel*. As we saw earlier, in Paul's day the Roman Empire was giving a counterfeit message of the "good news" of Caesar and the peace and safety his reign supposedly brought. But this is a very different kind of news—this is *better* news, the *best* news! This is news that changes everything. I'm convinced it's even better news than most of us have heard or dared to believe.

*Gospel* is such a small word to say, but such an enormous, grand, revolutionary word. There is so much bound up in it. First and foremost, it's good news because the gospel, according to Paul, is "from God." The gospel is God's message—a point Paul makes relentlessly clear, using the word *God* or *God's* 162 times in this one letter (in the English Standard Version)! The gospel is God's work. God has done all the heavy lifting. The gospel is not contingent on anything we've done or haven't done. It is all about what Jesus has done for us.

What happened to Paul himself demonstrates what the gospel always does: it changes us the exact moment we hear it spoken. The gospel brings salvation, wholeness, and life. The words of the gospel open up new possibilities. Its power is explosive, raw, and primal. The Greek word *dunamis* is the root word from which we get *dynamite*. It really does explode! The gospel is the dynamic of God, the dynamite of God.

But there is another dimension to this word in Greek; it also denotes a prescription. We all know the power of a prescription: How you can wake up, feel a scratchiness in your throat, and know the flu is coming on. As the day goes, you get more sore, and feverish, until by the afternoon you are positively miserable. When you've suffered enough, you drive to urgent care because you are desperate for a prescription—just a few simple words, often barely legible, scratched out on a small sheet of paper. But the scribbles on that tiny sheet of paper have the authority to change your life! Those few words have the power to make all the difference in your condition.

That is the gospel; it is God's prescription. We need only to take it once, and one dose is enough to change us forever, for all eternity. Contained in those small, dynamic words is the very healing of God. The gospel is God's power in verbal form! Its words change the temperature the moment we start to believe them.

## THE GOOD NEWS WAS NOT AN AFTERTHOUGHT

This good news was never an afterthought. The gospel is God's message, which "he promised beforehand through his prophets in the Holy Scriptures" (Rom. 1:2, NIV). Or as Paul will say later in Romans, we were "predestined to be conformed to the image of his Son" (8:29, NIV). God didn't create humans, react in shock and horror at their capacity to mess things up, freak out, and then call a huddle with Jesus and the Holy Spirit to come up with an emergency plan B in order to redeem us. God was never caught off guard by our failures. He created us in perfect love, knowing full well all the ways we would hurt ourselves and each other, not to mention all the ways we would violate His laws. And before any of it happened, even before the foundation of the earth, God already had a plan in place to get His sons and daughters back.

Long ago He decided to adopt you into His family. He took pleasure in planning this—it wasn't a headache or a heartache. He was so excited about you! He was excited to know you and for you to know Him. He was excited from the beginning about showing you all the beauty there is in Himself and His creation. He delights in you—not because of anything that you have done, but simply because you exist. He loves you precisely where you are and how you are; exactly as you were made. And nothing, nobody, anywhere or anytime can stop Him from loving you and pursuing you. He's been crazy about you every minute of your life, and all the minutes before you got to this one, too. It is the gospel that makes it possible for us to know this God of love. The gospel makes it possible because it is God's own plan that comes from God to us.

Since God knew you before you were born and had a plan for you from the beginning, He is able to see things in you that you cannot see in yourself. God sees you and knows you exactly where you are and how you are, and He loves you madly. That in and of itself is good news! But God doesn't just see you as you are; He also perceives what you can and will yet become. He starts with the end in mind!

You might be reading this and wondering if God loves you. You might be wondering if God could possibly see you or know you right where you are. This is part and parcel of the good news: God has *always* known you! God knew you before you were conceived. God knew about you, wanted you, and chose for you to be here, right now, reading these words. The circumstances of how you were conceived or how you got here simply do not matter. If you are here, you are here because God loves you and wants you.

Think about this: God *wants* you. He chooses you. He is choosing you with every breath. God has always wanted you and hovered over you, even in your darkest moments. In the words of the psalmist, "If I make my bed in [hell], you are there! If I take the wings of the morning and dwell in the uttermost parts of the sea, even there your hand shall lead me, and your right hand shall hold me" (Ps. 139:8–10). He has always known you, watched over you, and cared for you. You have never escaped the warmth of His loving presence, even in the lowest moment of your life. This love is inescapable and inexhaustible. It surrounds you, covers you, even as you read this. Love calls out for you by name. It was His plan all along to hold you close!

This gospel is not just for you. As Paul put it, the gospel will "bring about the obedience of faith for the sake of his name among all the nations" (Rom. 1:5). This gospel is for everyone—*everyone*! No one is left out—no matter who they are, what they've done, or where they come from; whether rich or poor, educated or uneducated; no matter what ethnicity, color, or what language they speak. The gospel transcends any and every human border and calls us from our respective families into the family of God. In a breathtaking statement for which we have no parallel in the ancient world, the same Paul wrote in Galatians that in Christ "There is neither Jew nor Greek, there is neither slave nor free, there is no male and female" (3:28). It doesn't matter who you are or where you come from. Grace makes no exceptions.

## THE GOOD NEWS IS BETTER THAN YOU THOUGHT IT WAS

The more I've become convinced that the gospel really is *the* good news, the more I've come to believe that it's not just good news for those who have a radical testimony and some colorful past fading in the rearview mirror. It's good news for those of us who are still in process, those of us who are still living in the messy middle. Paul's journey alone should tell us that grace is not for the faint of heart; it's not for the refined, but for rogues and rebels. Grace tamed and domesticated is no longer grace. At its core grace is wild; it refuses to be hemmed by either our human standards or our religious tradition.

Growing up I was raised to be responsible, work hard, and keep the rules, so when I became a Christian, I approached my faith with the same sense of responsibility and determination. As a pastor I applied that same ethic to my preaching and my concept of discipleship. Let's just say I had a view of grace that I've since come to see wasn't grace at all. When it comes to God's working in our own lives, and especially in the lives of others, it hasn't always been easy to grasp the way God not only puts up with broken people but also patiently works in their lives and even uses them to change the world! There has always been something messy about the grace of

God and the lives grace sovereignly disrupts—in His time and in our own.

Ask me what I want on vacation, and I will readily answer: a beach, a book, and a pillow. Few things are more relaxing for me than losing myself in a book while ocean waves rhythmically slap the beach. But while I was planning on losing myself on a winter trip to Mexico with my family, God was initiating a new phase in my understanding of grace. At the time I wasn't a Johnny Cash fan, but following his death in 2003 a number of books were written about his life, and I randomly began reading about the man in black. If you know anything about Cash, he didn't just sing about living hard—he actually did his share of hard living: marital affairs; on-again, off-again drug and alcohol addiction; and so on.

But the Cash I read about, for all of his struggles and failings, had grasped something of grace, too—or perhaps better said, grace had grasped ahold of him. He was a man well acquainted with the bottom, and it was there that God was waiting for him.

The most shocking thing about Johnny's story had nothing to do with his dark side or wild lifestyle. For somebody who had been taught, "I do my part, and God does His," Johnny's life shouted something different to me. His was a message more like "God does His part. Period." Whatever I had thought grace was before, I began to see that it was a whole lot bigger and a great deal wider than I had been led to believe.

In Cash's own words: "There was nothing left of me....I had drifted so far away from God and every stabilizing force in my life that I felt there was no hope....My separation from Him, the deepest and most ravaging of the various kinds of loneliness I'd felt over the years, seemed finally complete. It wasn't. I thought I'd left Him, but He hadn't left me. I felt something very powerful start to happen to me, a sensation of utter peace, clarity, and sobriety.... Then my mind started focusing on God."[1] What a remarkable picture of grace!

## THE GRACE TO BE FOUND
## ON SWERVING ROADS

I had an encounter with God early in my life that redirected my path and kept me from certain kinds of choices and pain. I am forever grateful for the grace that protected me from a path of self-destruction.

In my teens I came to Christ through an Assemblies of God church. A couple of years later the Lord called me into the ministry. Along the way part of my preparation for the ministry came by way of attending a Bible college. While I will always be indebted to the school I attended for much of the spiritual foundation it created in me, there was a lot of emphasis on religious performance and keeping the rules. As a result I'm sure I was more judgmental of people whose journey of grace was not so linear. But I've come to see now that the journey of the elder son (in Jesus' famous parable of the prodigal—which you'll remember is really about two lost sons!) to the heart of the father is actually no less miraculous than the journey of his prodigal brother! For the religious and the nonreligious, the saints and the ain'ts, it is still only grace that leads us home.

Holley Gerth wrote, "The road may be straight and narrow but we are not. We are the stragglers and drunkards weaving side to side."[2] I suppose the road toward grace always involves some swerving. The Damascus Road is a curvy road, and like Cash himself, we don't always walk the line. But the winding road can yet lead us home.

---

**For the religious and the nonreligious, the saints and the ain'ts, it is still only grace that leads us home.**

---

Some of us are still a little uncomfortable with a grace that walks on the wild side. But it is precisely because we are deeply broken people with all kinds of issues that a weak, watered-down, safe message of grace can never be enough to transform us. The kind of grace that changes us—the kind of grace that revolutionizes the world—is untamed, and for those who equate rules with righteousness, the grace Paul describes can seem to border on reckless.

Robert Farrar Capon, who uniquely grasps the undomesticated nature of grace, wrote about Luther's reformation.

> The Reformation was a time when people went blind-staggering drunk because they had discovered, in the dusty basement of late medievalism, a whole cellarful of fifteen-hundred-year-old, 200-proof grace—of bottle after bottle of pure distillate of Scripture that would convince anyone that God saves us single-handed. The Word of the Gospel, after all those centuries of believers trying to lift themselves into heaven by worrying about the perfection of their own bootstraps, suddenly turned out to be a flat announcement that the saved were home free even before they started.... Grace was to be drunk neat: no water, no ice, and certainly no ginger ale; neither goodness, nor badness, nor the

flowers that bloom in the spring of super-spirituality could be allowed to enter into the case.[3]

People sometimes wonder if this good news can be taken too far. The truth is, we can't possibly take the gospel any further than God already has! The good news is better than you thought it was. Grace gets messy because our lives are messy—and that's what God had in mind for us all along.

## Chapter 4

# THE BAD NEWS

For all have sinned and fall short of the glory of God.

—ROMANS 3:23

BECAUSE OF THE witness of God in the beauty of creation itself, and even within our own respective consciences, we know deep down that something within us is just not right. We know that we are ourselves complicit in the kind of world that chooses greed over justice, self over our neighbor, violence over God's place. We know we have all played a role in an unjust world where we are still an awfully long way from Jesus' vision of a people who value meekness, humility, and being poor in spirit over being powerful, beautiful, and successful. Because on some level we know we aren't in alignment with God's good purpose for creation, we (especially those of us who claim to be religious!) tend to manically find some way to justify ourselves—some way to make ourselves right (or righteous).

When I think of that kind of scrambling, I think about my son Brandon and his wife, Beth, taking a recent trip. They left the house in high spirits, drinking coffee in the car, their luggage packed and ready to go in the back. It wasn't until they got to the Branson, Missouri, airport that Brandon made a terrible discovery: his ID was not in his wallet. He didn't have time to go back to his house and get it. Frantically he began to look for loopholes to still make his flight. He googled on his phone and found out that you can sometimes get through airport security using mail with your address on it as a form of ID. So he madly tore through his car, where he found a few coffee-stained bills to take to security. Remarkably, the nice TSA folks in Branson let him through.

Brandon was doubtful that he would have the same luck getting through security on his return flight home, so he called a friend and had him break into his house, find his

ID, and overnight it to him while he was away, hoping to be ready for his return trip. When he got the package, his stomach dropped: he saw that his driver's license, now in hand, was actually expired, and had a hole punched through it! So even his ID was not valid. Somehow with that and his church employee ID card (hardly the kind of thing you'd expect TSA to take seriously) he made the return flight too! In many ways Brandon's story is a pretty wonderful illustration of mercy, which is largely what this book is about.

But for the purpose of this chapter, which is about how we can't have the good news until we've fully understood the bad news, Brandon's frantic search for a valid ID illustrates our shared human problem. We mostly try to charm our way out of any charges filed against us. We will scramble breathlessly for some shred of evidence, anything that might validate us. But over and over again, no matter how hard we flail, we don't have any credentials that will justify us.

We try to come to God on the basis of our own goodness and morality, hoping that we have somehow given enough to charity or made enough cookies for the PTA bake sale to be counted as "righteous." We may even still believe in some kind of judgment—it's just that, as Paul points out in Romans 2, we almost always think it's "the other guy" who deserves it! We compare ourselves with others we presume to be somehow morally worse off than we are ("well I may not be perfect, but at least I'm not like *him*," or "at least I'm not like *her!*"). No matter who you are or where you come from, everybody has somebody they can look down on. Our "righteousness" is based on a false sense of moral superiority that comes from scapegoating our neighbor as opposed to coming into humble dependence on a good God as our source. We "play God" with the people around us instead of coming to God in dependence, humility, and trust.

But at the end of the day, no matter how many good works we might stack up, we just don't measure up to God's standard of perfect love. Without grace we are still choosing ourselves and our own comfort and pleasure over God and our neighbor, in some form or another. That's why judgment is necessary and why judgment matters—because *we* matter, because our lives have weight.

Francis Spufford writes: "Taking the things people do wrong seriously is part of taking *them* seriously. It's part of letting their actions have weight. It's part of letting their actions *be* actions rather than just indifferent shopping choices; of letting their lives tell a life-story, with consequences, and losses, and gains, rather than just being a flurry of events. It's part of letting them be real enough to be worth loving, rather than just attractive or glamorous or pretty or charismatic or cool."[1]

## THE WRATH OF GOD

If Romans is our field guide to grace, it's easy to see how folks can get tangled up in it. This same book that lays out the beauty of God in such radical ways also has plenty to say about the wrath of God. I can't think of a single person who likes that word. When we hear the word *wrath*, we immediately think of an unhinged emotional response—irrational, uncontrolled, vindictive, cruel, selfish, or harsh. We frame God's attributes in the context of human personality and project human attributes to God.

For the many people who have attended toxic churches or have a heartbreaking story of an abusive parent or spouse, it's the kind of word that can trigger a great deal of pain. In our context it might conjure an image of an alcoholic father who batters his wife or his children—an angry, erratic, out-of-control person who is taking out his angst on the people around him. Some people can barely even conceive of God as Father precisely because their earthly fathers have been so horrible to them.

Those scenarios are not descriptive of the God who comes to save us; they describe the kinds of hell God comes to save us from. God is not abusive, and not an abuser! God has nothing in common with people who harm children. In fact, it is precisely because God is so passionate about His children that He is so radically opposed to sin and evil—He cannot help but abhor that which brings His children harm.

The wrath of God is not emotional, petty, or punitive. It has nothing to do with "rage." Rather, the wrath of God, in Romans, is bound up in the natural consequences of certain kinds of choices—as Paul will put it later in the book, "the wages of sin is death" (6:23). God's primary job is not to go around making sure everybody gets what they deserve—in fact, God is constantly interrupting the natural cycle of cause and effect with grace! Nevertheless we get to choose the kind of life we want and the kind of world we want to live in. As much as God is committed to seek and save that which is lost, God is also passionate about preserving human freedom—He won't drag anybody kicking and screaming into some kind of eternal bliss without their consent. If we want to choose selfishness over love for God and for our neighbors, inevitably choosing the type of life that brings violence and division to the world for which Christ died (rather than healing), we are given that option.

---

God's primary job is not to go around making
sure everybody gets what they deserve—in
fact, God is constantly interrupting the natural
cycle of cause and effect with grace!

---

Human selfishness always leads to pain and brokenness
for the sons and daughters God so desperately loves, which
is precisely why God remains actively opposed and wholly
hostile to evil. He refuses to condone it or to come to terms
with it. The justice of God is not somehow opposite of the
love of God—it is rather a manifestation of it. We live in
a world where people are exploited, oppressed, and abused,
and all that is exploitive, oppressive, and abusive must be
brought under judgment for things to be made right. And
that is what God's justice is all about—in the skillful phrase
of N. T. Wright's, "the world being put to rights."[2] Isaiah
prophesied about it when he talked about the time when
the mountains would be brought low and the valleys lifted
high. The world as we know it is not just. It is not equal. It
is not fair. Inevitably, a God who is relentlessly committed
to loving and restoring His creation must judge the world.
As Paul demonstrates in Romans 8, creation itself is actually
crying out for God's justice to come!

## WHY WE ARE WITHOUT EXCUSE

To judge is to call people into account. This is a hard thing
to talk about because we know that people mostly mean
well and we don't always know why we do the things we do.
Keep in mind that the whole point of the Book of Romans
(and the story of Scripture in general) is to reveal God's

extravagant grace! But according to Paul there are things we can be held accountable for precisely because we do know more than we might let on. This is the argument he makes in Romans 1—that creation itself testifies to the glory and splendor of God in ways that all people can plainly see and recognize. This is why we are "without excuse" (v. 20) when it comes to the judgment of God.

As I've heard it said, "God has left large footprints throughout creation." Creation itself bears witness to the splendor and majesty of God. Whenever we look at the stars, the rhythm of the seasons, or the poetry of God in *life itself*—all of creation declares, "There is a God!" To put it another way, the earth itself testifies to God's goodness.

The stunning, spectacular craftsmanship of the cosmos is apparent in every detail. Even if we don't look any further into the splendor of creation than our own bodies, the intricate handiwork on display in them is awe-inspiring. The dazzling scope, size, and spectacle of creation—the design of the planet, its atmosphere, and its inhabitants…*screams* to us of a Designer. The staggering beauty of nature alone necessitates that we believe in a Creator.

In Paul's shorthand account of creation and the fall (Rom. 1:18–32) he makes the case that instead of worshipping the Creator, people chose to worship the creation—in other words, we chose idolatry. And it really doesn't matter what the idols are, because the outcome is always the same: idolatry means we end up choosing something else over God. We want something or someone to fulfill us, to give us purpose and meaning in a way only God can. Our idols are things or people we "use" to gratify ourselves instead of looking to the only One who can satisfy us. We choose alienation and separation, not only from God but also from the people around us.

In verses 29–31 Paul lists some of the unhealthy things we do—ranging from subtly destructive to openly horrible—when we choose an idol over the Creator: "all manner of unrighteousness, evil, covetousness, malice. They are full of envy, murder, strife, deceit, maliciousness. They are gossips, slanderers, haters of God, insolent, haughty, boastful, inventors of evil, disobedient to parents, foolish, faithless, heartless, ruthless." The individual idols and actions are not the point so much. The point is that when we choose something or someone over God, we are left high and dry to the consequences of our actions; we are left to sexual and philosophical confusion, left unsure of who we are and what we were put here to do. It's a hard pill to swallow, but no one is exempt from this kind of idol worship. As Paul builds to a crescendo in Romans 3, "All have sinned and fall short of the glory of God" (v. 23).

In response to this, God does not lose His temper or fly off the handle. God simply allows us to have what we choose. It is not God who banishes us; we banish ourselves. This is the genius of C. S. Lewis' famous book *The Great Divorce*. In it, no one is in hell because God sends them there, but rather hell is locked from the inside. "There are only two kinds of people in the end," Lewis concludes, "those who say to God, 'Thy will be done,' and those to whom God says, in the end, '*Thy* will be done.'"[3] Hell exists not because of some divine desire for torment but because of God's insistence on free will.

## THE BAD NEWS BEFORE
## THE GOOD NEWS

Keep in mind that Paul is both the recipient and the apostle of God's radical grace! It is not that he is especially cynical or pessimistic about the human condition—Paul is just realistic. As we read elsewhere in his letters, Paul was a Jew of Jews, a devout man who did everything within his power to honor the Law, to keep all the rules. And yet he knew from his own first-person experience that his moralism never actually changed his heart; it didn't transform him into a different kind of person or make him into something new. Only grace can do that!

---

When you get to the end of yourself,
the story of God's outrageous grace
can officially begin in you.

---

This is why the good news can't really be good news to us until we first understand the bad news. We are far more prone to deception (especially self-deception), selfishness, and outright meanness than we know. That bent toward self runs right down to the bone. And the only way we can really experience radical transformation is if we completely give up on the self-justifying business, the being-right-in-our-own-eyes business, and the comparison business, and throw ourselves completely, utterly, desperately into the arms of the God who loves us at our worst.

God isn't looking for qualified people. Nobody is qualified for something as absurd and wonderful as grace! God looks for people who can admit their qualifications don't matter.

When you get to the end of yourself, the story of God's outrageous grace can officially begin in you.

Yes, we are more lost than we know. But we are loved beyond our wildest reckoning.

## Chapter 5

# THE GIFT OF A LIFETIME

For if Abraham was justified by works, he has something to boast about, but not before God. For what does the Scripture say? "Abraham believed God, and it was counted to him as righteousness."

—ROMANS 4:2–3

CHILDREN ARE CAPABLE of a kind of unfettered honesty that adults can rarely match. My son David has three boys and one baby girl, whom we adore. Her name is Henley, but David calls her Boo. She's a unique mix of lovable sweetness and daredevil. I can easily picture her as the first woman to win the Indy 500. Not long ago she was exhibiting her daring side by hitting one of her older brothers. David sat down with her and asked, "Boo, why did you hit your brother?" Comically she looked at him with a glint in her eye and said, *Because I wanted to.* It was hilarious because she's cute and delightful, but she answered like a cold-blooded gangster!

But beyond the humor it is a tragically realistic assessment of much of the harm we end up inflicting on each other—we do things *simply because we want to*. This is the heart of the sin problem we explored in the last chapter.

In light of our endless propensity to mess things up even when our intentions are good, along with all our inventive ways of causing harm to ourselves and to each other, we need a radical solution. Surely forgiveness is part of it, yes—but it cannot be all of it. What we need is not just to have our record expunged, but something much more radical—we are in need of nothing short of utter transformation.

Romans remains such an explosive book precisely because it contains the radical answer to sin, the root dilemma of our species. That solution can be summed up in a single word: *justification*.

## AN UNSPEAKABLE GIFT

We have glimpsed the darkness, not only in the last chapter but even more so within ourselves, if we've really been paying attention to what our lives and our own hearts tell us. Without the darkness we could not appreciate the blinding splendor of the light. The stark backdrop of the bad news only makes the glory of the good news shine all the brighter. Everything we've looked at thus far, while important, is really only context through which we come to see the staggering beauty of the gift that God freely offers to humanity through Jesus Christ. Justification is the gift of a lifetime; the gift that can change how we see God, ourselves, and the world. Justification. So much of the Christian faith is bound up in those syllables—it is a word that contains a story as vast as Scripture itself.

But before we unpack the word *justification*, let's start with a smaller and more familiar word and chew it slowly: for the apostle Paul, justification is a *gift*. It is all a gift, it has always been a gift, and it is only a gift. This is counterintuitive, as so many of us think we can work our way into heaven. Yet precisely because justification is a gift, it cannot be earned— no matter how hard you try to be a good person, no matter how much money you give to hurricane relief, no matter how hard you try to be nice. You cannot work your way into heaven, no matter how hard you work. There is nothing you can do to earn justification.

Many Christians believe they must do certain things in order to be accepted by God. It is good and right to be a member of a church. Engaging spiritual disciplines like prayer, fasting, and Bible study can be tremendously beneficial. But no matter how much you read your Bible, weep, try to do more, give more, be more; no matter how hard you try to extract yourself from your darkest addictions—none of that can make you "worthy" of salvation. As Paul made so clear in Romans 3, none of us are worthy!

Because we have so many reasons to need God's mercy to cover our past, forgiveness is certainly a key component of justification. People often, and appropriately, speak of salvation in terms of Christ forgiving our sin. Forgiveness is wonderful—but justification hardly stops there. For the apostle Paul justification is not *just* a word for a one-time legal, judicial act (getting a verdict of not guilty), but a word for everything that happens from the moment we first place our trust in Jesus until the day we are somehow mysteriously transformed into His likeness. It is a word that encapsulates an entire, sweeping, life-altering journey; a way of being in the world that changes the whole trajectory of our existence. Simply put, justification is the key to everything in the life of faith.

## SALVATION IS A PROCESS

While a relationship with Jesus has to begin at a particular point in time for all of us, it is not a one-time event. Salvation is actually a three-part process. "I *was* saved." That is justification. "I *am being* saved." That is sanctification, the gradual process of the inward desires and orientation of our hearts being transformed by love as we adopt the character of Christ. "I *will* be saved" is glorification, the part of our salvation that is yet to come, in which we are fully conformed to the image of Christ. In the language of 1 John, "what we will be has not yet been made known. But we know that when Christ appears, we shall be like him" (3:2, NIV).

If salvation is the gift of a lifetime, justification is the first box we get to open; and it is the key to understanding all the others. Everything else that happens in a life with God is supposed to come as a natural extension of gratitude to God in response to this free gift.

For Paul in Romans justification is *the act of God whereby He forgives the unsaved person's sin and imputes/credits/assigns to them the righteousness of Christ when through faith they believe. First and foremost—yes, God does forgive our sins!* That is no small thing. Imagine coming into the court of heaven knowing our own righteousness is like "filthy rags," in the language of Isaiah 64:6 (NIV), and having all the charges dropped! That alone is unfathomable. If salvation didn't entail anything else but the forgiveness of our sins, that would be reason enough to party forever.

But as wonderful as this news is, it is *not* the full extent of the good news (even though a lot of churches and Christians stop here). Forgiveness is about letting go of a debt, letting someone off the hook for some wrong they have inflicted upon us, and refusing to seek retribution. But it is completely possible to forgive someone yet still not experience intimacy with them, to say, "I forgive you, I won't take you to court; I won't seek punishment," and yet not restore the relationship with the person who wronged us or the person we wronged.

While Paul does use courtroom language to talk about sin, it is much more serious than a legal problem. Even if our individual sins were forgiven, we would still be unrighteous, if forgiveness was all that we were offered. Our sin problem is far more profound than any particular actions; the whole is greater than the sum of the parts. In the words of David in Psalm 51:5, "In sin did my mother conceive me." Sin is not just descriptive of particular acts but a way of being in the world without God—a way of attempting to live our lives without being connected to our divine source.

As the Eastern Orthodox tradition has always understood well, and John Wesley brought to bear for those of us in the Western Church, sin is not just about actions that need to be pardoned, but a sickness that needs to be healed. God isn't content to just declare us to be righteous (though in Christ He *does* declare us to be righteous!); God wants us to actually *be* holy, which is just another way of saying He wants to make us whole.

For the apostle Paul, then, forgiveness is just the beginning of what it means to be "saved," not the end. Once we place our trust in Christ, God begins the process of sanctifying us. This doesn't have anything to do with becoming moralistic or trying to prove to God that we are worthy of His mercy. No! It's about falling deeper in love with Jesus until our hearts are perfectly His. It's the gradual process of coming to love God more than we love anything or anyone else, and slowly beginning to work out the implications of that love in every aspect of our lives. It's not about legalism...it's about love!

This is where spiritual disciplines and practices become so important in the life of faith; not so we can earn or get more of God—when you place your faith in Christ, you've already got as much God in you as you could ever want! It's about letting God get more of us, letting God into every nook and cranny; letting God into not just our behaviors but also our desires, affections, and motivations. Sanctification, really, is just about allowing grace to saturate us all the way on the inside. And this process of sanctification, which begins the moment you first come to God in childlike faith, will continue until the day you die. You never stop learning, growing, and changing!

But then finally, in Romans 8, Paul talks about glorification. That is what happens when we die, or when King Jesus comes to earth to make things right—we are actually, entirely transformed into the image of Christ! That's what we have to look forward to—the day when everything in us is like everything in Him, without any barrier or distinction.

This may sound like bad news if you are a perfectionist who feels the need to get everything right as soon as you come out of the gate. But the gospel makes it clear that we are not right and we are not going to get it right on our own. While we are in this process of ongoing transformation, there will be many moments when we will get discouraged or feel like we take two steps forward, then three steps back. Growth and transformation in grace is hardly a neat, linear process! But here's the really amazing news: that transformation is not up to us. And as faithless as we can be at times, the One who saves is forever faithful. In the words of Paul elsewhere in the New Testament, "He who began a good work in you will bring it to completion at the day of Jesus Christ" (Phil. 1:6).

The good work God has started in you He has already promised to complete—and you can take that to the bank!

## Chapter 6

# BY FAITH FROM BEGINNING TO END

[Abraham was] fully convinced that God was able to do what he had promised.

—ROMANS 4:21

**S**EVERAL YEARS AGO, while traveling through Europe, Debbie and I visited one of the most famed sites in all of church history as we stood where the German monk turned Protestant Reformer, Martin Luther, nailed his Ninety-Five Theses to the door of the church at Wittenburg. It's hard to overstate the impact of the theological revolution he sparked with his pen and his hammer. Like the apostle Paul before him, Luther was radical for grace. His own tumultuous interior journey with self-doubt and condemnation had driven him to a revelatory experience of God's mercy, and he was never the same. Also like his hero, Paul, he had walked his own sort of road to Damascus, and once you see grace in all its splendor, it is impossible to unsee.

The central cry of the reformation he triggered was *sola fide*—faith alone. Luther famously called this the doctrine or article by which the church stands or falls. As we walk our own respective roads, I would add that our own lives will stand or fall based on what we do with these very truths.

In Romans 4, Paul shows us the centrality of faith for a life with God. His own faith is certainly grounded in his belief that Jesus is Israel's long-awaited Messiah, the Anointed One. But writing to an audience who, like most of the earliest followers of Jesus, was likely still comprised more of those who had come to believe in Jesus from within the Jewish tradition than those who had come from outside of it, Paul makes a strong claim. While he believed in the particularity of Jesus as God's Son, he makes the case that faith, and only faith, has always been the only thing God was ever looking for—even in the stories of the remarkable patriarchs and matriarchs of Jewish Scripture.

## MANY SONS HAD FATHER ABRAHAM

As we've glimpsed something of the magnitude of grace, this is the point at which it might all sound a little too good to be true. God promises to do all of that? Where is the catch? What's in the fine print? What am I leaving out?

Well, God does require one thing of us in order to receive this free gift of justification. And to illustrate this, the apostle Paul in Romans goes all the way back to the beginning of the Jewish story, to Israel's first bona fide rock star—the man who started it all: good old Father Abraham. Do you remember him? If you went to Sunday school as a kid, you probably heard all about Father Abraham and his many sons through the ever-popular children's ditty. If you know the song, don't worry—I will not require you to raise your right arm, nor your left arm, to nod your head, nor sit down (partly because I get these lyrics mixed up with "The Hokey Pokey").

You have to remember that Abraham—along with Moses and David—was one of the famous heroes of the Old Testament, legends whose stories are told over and over again by devout Jews. There are many wonderful stories about the things these heroic figures got right (and also quite a few stories of what they got wrong, by the way). But according to Paul, the reason God was able to so powerfully use Abraham—promising him a great name, a great nation, many sons and daughters, and a legacy so profound that ultimately through him "all the families of the earth would be blessed"—was for one reason, and one reason only: *Abraham believed.*

That's right. You didn't misread that last sentence, and there is no fine print. Like all the Old Testament patriarchs,

Abraham got about as much wrong as he did right. But the thing he got right, he got *really right*. Abraham took God at His word. He completely trusted in God's promises.

Sure, Abraham was mostly obedient. When God told him to go, he went. When God told him to sacrifice his son, he was willing to do that too. (Even though ultimately God did not require that of him—as it turns out, God is actually not into sacrifices, just broken hearts in need of His grace!) But the thing he got so right in God's eyes wasn't in the obedience, per se—he still fell short of doing that perfectly. Abraham *believed*!

The early church deviates in significant ways from traditional forms of Jewish worship, particularly with regard to how Christians should keep Torah (the Law), as Paul addresses at length in many letters. But the more striking thing about the relationship between these stories of God is not the discontinuity between them, but the continuity. The story of Jesus as Israel's Messiah is very much a continuation of the story of God and the Jewish people.

The victory of God in the cross and resurrection of Jesus changes so much for us, setting us free from sin, Satan, and ourselves once and for all. But Paul maintains that the way to God in both halves of the story of God has always been faith, still is faith, and always will be faith. Abraham was a great man in Jewish tradition. But according to Paul, the thing that made him great was simply this: when God spoke to him, he believed what God said. He listened, he took God's voice seriously, and he did what God asked him to do. That is all. To quote Romans 4:21, he was "fully convinced that God was able to do what he had promised."

# THE OBJECT OF FAITH...
## IS NOT FAITH!

We are endlessly creative at making things harder for ourselves than we need to. It is perfectly easy to turn the idea of faith into a legalistic enterprise that is still contingent on our efforts. "Do I have enough faith? Is it pure enough? I think my trust in God is only at 67 percent. Is that high enough? How could I get to 73 percent? Do I need to wish harder?" The trouble with how a lot of us think about our faith is that the emphasis often lands more on the *our* than the *faith*. If the emphasis is on *your* faith, regardless of how much or little *you* have, the focus is still on *you*. Even faith can become a kind of navel-gazing exercise, a way of taking your temperature every few minutes.

Ironically there have been expressions, particularly in the American church, where faith actually has us as the object rather than God as the object. Faith is supposed to be a way of rest, of giving up our need to control the world around us. But it can instead become just another kind of work where we are still doing the heavy lifting instead of God. But the object of faith is not faith. The object of faith is *God*. Faith can't be found by looking deeper inward, but by looking outside of ourselves. In the words of Hebrews 12:2 (NIV), "fixing our eyes on Jesus, the pioneer and perfecter of faith." Faith is about locking our gaze on Jesus, not on some inner faith tank.

So long as the attention is still on ourselves rather than Jesus, the life of faith is always going to be an uphill battle. Like Jesus walking out on the water in the midst of a terrible storm and calling to Peter to step out of the boat to meet Him, God comes to us and calls us, bidding us to step out of a life of false security and meet Him. We aren't called *out of* the wild, but *into* the wild; not *out of* the storm, but *into* the storm. But in that story, moments after Peter becomes the first human being (who is not also God-in-flesh) to walk on water, he takes his gaze off Jesus for a moment and begins to sink. It's easy to do: we start a walk with Jesus based on simple, childlike trust and an unadorned, sincere cry of "I believe!" But when the storm is raging around us and within us and we lose sight of Jesus, we start to feel ourselves slipping.

When we struggle to find faith within ourselves, the answer is not to self-generate more faith. It simply cannot be done! Faith does not originate with us. Rather, the King James Version of Hebrews 12:2 says that Jesus Himself is "the author and the finisher of our faith." Other translations say He is the founder or pioneer and perfecter of our faith. There is only one place where faith gets perfected, and it's in Him. Where does faith come from? *The source of faith and strength of faith comes from the author of faith!*

## WHY FAITH?

Have you ever wondered why faith is so central to the Christian journey—why it is given to us as the only means of knowing God? In his book *A Body of Divinity* the Puritan pastor and writer Thomas Watson asked this same question 350 years ago: Why is it that God uses faith as that vehicle for justification? In response he wrote, "Because of God's purpose. He has appointed this grace to be justifying; and he does it, because faith is a grace that takes a man off himself, and gives all the honor to Christ and free grace."[1] After writing this he quotes part of Romans 4:20, "Strong in faith, giving glory to God."

*That* is why faith is so central to the plan of salvation—it brings glory to God. It displays just how glorious God really is. Think about when Jesus rode into Jerusalem on what we call Palm Sunday, just a week before the crowds would turn on Him and crucify Him. It was the kind of processional you would have for a king. But Jesus did not come into the city riding on a horse in the way that kings do. Jesus instead came riding on a humble, borrowed donkey. The animal that He chose to ride was not beautiful or powerful; there is no danger of a beast of burden such as a donkey getting the glory! The only power and beauty on display were in the King Himself. In the same spirit we are also chosen to be conduits or vessels of the glory of God. And for similar reasons we know that when God chooses to work in and through us—in all of our fragility and brokenness—there is no danger of us getting any of the glory that rightfully belongs only to God!

Bringing glory to God is the very reason we exist. It is our *telos*, the end for which we were created. It is why we are here. We were created to bring God glory, and faith is what best demonstrates God's glory—no wonder it is precisely through faith that our lives can have a sense of purpose, order, orientation, and meaning.

## TRUSTING THE GOOD CHARACTER OF GOD

Faith, via Romans 4:21 (NIV), is "being fully persuaded that God had power to do what he had promised." Faith is the confidence that God is powerful enough to do what He said and trustworthy to keep His word. Faith doesn't have anything to do with coming up with predetermined outcomes and then holding God hostage to them, as if God is our genie in the bottle. People often start the life of faith assuming it will give them more certainty. The truth is, a life of faith is not a way of more certainty, but less! It does not mean we will know more about the path ahead or understand exactly where we are now—it is about *trust*, not knowledge. It is more a heart-knowing than a head-knowing. It is not contingent on anything about our lives going a particular way, for good or for ill.

Even when God speaks to us or moves us in a very clear way, that doesn't mean faith always comes easy. Abraham himself, this heroic exemplar of faith, "against all hope...in hope believed" (Rom. 4:18, NIV). What is hope against hope? It is when you have no reason to hope and yet, inexplicably, there is hope—not based on what you see, not based on what you feel, not based on what you are being told by people around you. When none of those places seem to have anything for you, against that backdrop, you place all you've got in the same place Abraham did "as he had been told." This is not a cheesy, look-on-the-sunny-side-of-life kind of hope. This is hope that can seem irrational; it is hope without any evidence of what you hope for, insofar as seeing with your human eyes. It transcends logic, reason, and knowledge of "the facts." Hope against hope is when you have nothing to go on but the word of God, and it is enough.

When you take a situation that you have no hope for and give it to God, you enlarge people's view of God's grandeur. That is what Abraham did when he trusted God to be true to His promise to give Abraham and Sarah a baby even though they were both already well past their child-bearing years.

Faith is not denial; it's not burying your head in the sand, refusing to look at the harsh realities of the world you live in. It doesn't mean you deny the grim facts of the situation—just as Abraham didn't deny the reality of his aged body! Faith does not require you to go blind; it is just a different way of seeing.

Faith doesn't give us a script or a map to follow, or necessarily any clear instructions as to exactly where we are going. In fact, if Abraham is our frame of reference for faith, God told Abraham to gather his things, pack up his family, and simply go, without telling him anything about where he was going or how he would get there! Life takes all of us places we never thought we would be taken. In the words of Jesus to Peter, the events of life can "lead you where you do not want to go" (John 21:18, NIV).

But faith has nothing to do with any particular destination— faith is about *trusting the character of God*. There are plenty of things we do not know about the path, but we know we can trust the heart of the One who guides us along it. We rarely know where we are going—and we aren't supposed to. The thing that we can know, and must know, is that *God is good* and He can be trusted. Faith always looks beyond the problem to the promise, and beyond the promise to *the person*.

It was this kind of faith—this relentless trust in the goodness of God against all the odds—that was credited to Abraham as righteousness. He was not a perfect man, just a trusting one. His strength was not his own character, but his trust in the character of God.

> Faith always looks beyond the problem to the promise, and beyond the promise to the person.

As it was for Abraham, faith makes the experience of all God's goodness available to you. You don't have to earn the promises of God. You don't have to bargain or barter for them. You cannot deserve or be worthy of them. The only thing you can do—and the only thing you are asked to do—is receive them. Martin Luther called it the Great Exchange.

- Jesus' perfection in exchange for your sin
- Jesus' suffering in exchange for your salvation
- Jesus' faultlessness in exchange for your freedom

No wonder when Luther saw the truth of this for what it is, it made him into a revolutionary. Perhaps grace might yet make radicals of us all.

## ALL GOD WANTS FROM YOU

If you want to know what God asks of you, this is it—nothing more or less than God wanted from Abraham: God wants your *faith*. God wants your trust. God wants you to take Him at His word.

God doesn't want you to beg. God doesn't want you to cry buckets of tears. God doesn't want you to crawl across broken glass to show you are sorry. God isn't asking for you to show initiative or prove that you "really mean business." God offers you everything in Christ, and the only thing

He asks in return is one small, simple question: "Will you trust Me?"

What exactly can you give to the God who has everything? You don't have anything He wants, certainly not anything He needs. As it turns out, God has never been primarily interested in anything you might do for Him. God wants you—even though you have nothing to bring to the table— because the essence of the gospel is what He has done, not what you could do. Without anything to commend you but His love for you, He invites you to come simply by faith and find He has provided everything.

In the words of the old hymn:

> Just as I am, without one plea
> But that Thy blood was shed for me,
> And that Thou bid'st me come to Thee,
> O Lamb of God, I come! I come![2]

## Chapter 7

# PEACE WITH GOD

Therefore, since we have been justified by faith, we have peace with God through our Lord Jesus Christ.

—Romans 5:1

Too MANY CHRISTIANS live in fear. They live an unsettled spiritual existence plagued with the nagging sense that they might not actually be saved. Every time an altar call is given or a gospel appeal is made, deep down they feel they might need to pray "the prayer" all over again. After all, since the last time they "received Jesus," things haven't gone that well. They entertained lust in their hearts or struggled with outbursts of anger. Surely their sinful missteps mean they have fallen from grace and their relationship with God has been compromised. So again and again they find themselves believing they need to be re-saved. Maybe this time it will take. Maybe this time they can really be sure. Maybe this will be the time when their salvation really begins to stick.

Isn't there something in the Bible somewhere about how if you get it wrong, it negates every bit of growth or goodness you've experienced up until that point, and now the divine umpire makes you begin at the starting line all over again? Isn't that how the spiritual life works?

Shockingly and mercifully, nothing remotely like that actually appears in the pages of Scripture. God does not make you start over every time you make a mistake. You do not have to ask God to save you over and over again just to make sure it "took." There is something about the radical simplicity of salvation and our own innate sense of unworthiness that nudges us to disbelieve that God's grace has staying power even when we fail.

Some people struggle with the assurance of their salvation their entire lives to the point of real psychological damage. When you've come up under preaching, however well-intentioned, that leads you to believe salvation is based on your consistent good behavior, you begin to view salvation as a tenuous, fragile thing. You could be as quickly and easily lost as you could be saved, and live every waking moment looking for the reset button. Feeling that kind of uncertainty about your soul can infect every area of your life, making you constantly second-guess yourself. It can sabotage your joy and sap your confidence, infusing anxiety into almost everything you do.

At this point in my life I'm convinced we experience this kind of constant anxiety about the state of our souls because we simply fail to grasp what a profound work God has already accomplished for us in justification. Our own humanity may always be feeble and fragile, but what God has accomplished in our salvation is anything but!

Romans 5:1 is a significant hinge point for the entire book: "*Therefore*, since we have been justified by faith, we have peace with God through our Lord Jesus Christ" (emphasis added). Thus far Paul has established the universality of the sin problem and the lengths to which God has gone to address sin through the gift of justification. Now Paul will unpack the riches of a life lived on the other side of justification, the treasures to be excavated now that our salvation is firmly established.

But we won't be able to mine and explore all these riches if we are still looking back over our shoulder, still always going back to square one. When you are in Christ, peace with God is not a flickering, glimmering moment—it is an established fact that changes the trajectory of your journey forever.

## THE ONE THING THAT
## DOESN'T CHANGE

Through the free gift of justification, everything about us changes. While justification is the first step in the process of salvation, it culminates with us being fully conformed to the image of Jesus, the implications of this step are enormous! Our very identity is altered—old names and labels are stripped from us, and we are now only known as beloved sons and daughters of God. But while everything has already changed, that doesn't mean your feelings will always get the memo. In the words of Henri Nouwen, "One of the tragedies of our life is that we keep forgetting who we are."[1] And indeed the moments will come when we forget this radical transformation God has wrought in us.

The people of God are not less likely than other people to contend with cancer or car accidents. Our circumstances will change as the weather changes, and the elements will try our very souls. Especially under stress and fatigue we will not always act out of our deepest sense of identity—we will not always readily remember who God says we are in Christ. Justified people still fail and falter and struggle at times to be consistent. We live in a world where so much changes so rapidly. If we have lived long enough, we have experienced dramatic changes in our relationships—sometimes people have disappointed or failed us; sometimes we have done the disappointing. Not only are our own feelings tossed at sea, in a constant state of flux based on storms in the world outside of us and storms in the world within us, but the way other people feel about us constantly shifts, too.

But for all the things about our lives that can and will change, justification changes the facts of our existence once and for all. A real transaction has taken place in which our status with God has been completely and irrevocably altered. You could think of justification as a legal, binding, forensic transaction in the court of love, where peace with God has been forever established!

As an emotional reality peace is a feeling as fleeting as any other. Sometimes we feel at peace, and sometimes we don't. Everything from the twenty-four-hour news cycle to the chemical rhythms of our bodies, songs on the radio, weather, traffic, and whether or not our sports team won on Sunday affects our conscious sense of peace (or lack thereof). That is why we must understand that the peace of God established in us through Christ is not a *feeling*; it's a *fact*.

Feelings rise and fall like waves throughout the day. How God feels about you never changes. Relationships come and go. God won't leave you or forsake you, no matter who leaves or who stays. When you get the job or lose the job, when you change the relationship status on your Facebook profile—the peace of God never wavers. God's peace is not mental tranquility. It doesn't have anything to do with positive feelings, or the lack of them. It is not based on our experience but on the evidence. It has nothing to do with what we feel and everything to do with what we know.

## THE WAR IS OVER

We are born into war, each of us children of a cosmic conflict. A battle between God and Satan, light and darkness, evil and good, started long before we got here. We are all children of Adam, which Paul explains at length in Romans 5. We are all products of the fall. Sin is not just a matter of wrong individual choices we make but something in our very

DNA. "In sin did my mother conceive me," David wrote in Psalm 51:5. We are all crooked in our depths. Still very much created in the image of God—yes! The image of God in us was never lost. But it has been marred by sin, by this inward bent toward self. Because of this, there is a war not only around us, but a war within us—a war between true self and false self, between truth and lies.

---

## Peace has nothing to do with what we feel and everything to do with what we know.

---

But just as decisively as all children of Adam are born into conflict, where the fall of one man affects us all, even more so is the resurrection power of Christ now released into all those who believe in Him! This is the heart of Paul's argument in Romans 5. Sin, according to Paul, made us enemies with God—not because God ever stopped loving us, but because God actively opposes evil and refuses to cooperate with it. But while we were still sinners—still the enemies of God—Christ died for us. On the cross Jesus did exactly what He taught us to do: He forgave His enemies. Even as He breathed His last breath, He was still extending forgiveness: "Father, forgive them, for they know not what they do" (Luke 23:34).

Now to those who have said yes to the God fully revealed in Christ: "If, while we were God's enemies, we were reconciled to him through the death of his Son, how much more, having been reconciled, shall we be saved through his life!" (Rom. 5:10, NIV). The war is over. Reconciliation is now our only reality.

Elsewhere Paul will tell us to "work out [our] own salvation with fear and trembling" (Phil. 2:12). The idea is not "go off on your own and figure out your salvation" or "figure out if you are saved." Rather the idea is to allow the natural implications of what God has done for you in Christ to be worked out in your daily lives—literally allow it to work its way outward. Let it work its way into everything you say, everything you do, and everything you are. Let the inward work God has already accomplished for you in Christ be worked *out*, into every nook and cranny of your life. That's what Romans 5–8 outlines for us—it explains how the work God has already done now can be "worked out" in and through our lives, and ultimately out into the world.

## PAST, PRESENT, AND FUTURE

One of the revelations that has most altered my life has been this simple but revolutionary truth: Jesus died for all our sins—past, present, and future. While Jesus was crucified at a particular moment in history, history does not hold Him down. His sacrifice is not constricted by space and time. Scripture declares that Jesus is the Lamb of God "slain from the foundation of the world" (Rev. 13:8, NKJV). Because God made this provision for us before there was even an "us," the crucifixion of Jesus is a past event for all of us. He sacrificed Himself not just before we ever sinned, but before we were even conceived! That sacrifice did not just anticipate the sins we would commit before we woke up to the reality of Jesus; that sacrifice anticipated any and every kind of misstep you will make today. And not today only—that sacrifice anticipated any failure of yours that is yet to come!

When we do not grasp the fact that our past, present, and

future were dealt with once and for all on the cross, we are left with a salvation that by and large depends on us rather than on Him. Salvation is not contingent on my consistency or lack thereof, my capacity to keep the rules, or any other human effort. The weight of all my sin and shame was placed on His shoulders, not on mine. He accomplished the work and invites us now to rest in Him and the gift of salvation He has won for us by His own blood.

The most common objection to this kind of teaching is from people who are afraid that believing this way will cause some people to abuse the teaching of grace, to sin as much as they want since all their sins are forgiven. Paul himself anticipated this kind of response from his early readers from the churches in Rome. (See Romans 6.) Yes, if grace is preached with power, people will inevitably abuse it. But that doesn't change the hard, rock-solid truth of salvation.

From the moment we first place faith in Christ, God begins a work of changing our hearts to be more inclined to His own. Our affections become more sensitive to that which pleases Him and that which offends Him. Our desires begin to conform to the desires of Jesus.

If someone cavalierly continues to choose a path that grieves the Spirit of God without any remorse or change in direction, it is doubtful they have placed their faith in God's work. The frightening reality is that they have forfeited real peace for the false peace that quiets God's voice and offers no assurance. You can certainly have a real encounter with Jesus and still struggle with sin, but you won't be indifferent about it because you are growing to love God more. Sin won't separate you from the love of God, but everything in you is being rewired to make you want to please God. When you do fall, you get up, brush the dust off, and keep on walking. You can do this with confidence because peace with God is not a feeling; it's a fact.

For those of us who love God, our path will be marked by strong steps forward, random detours, and sometimes outright steps back. The path is not always linear, but it always leads to a fuller revelation of God in Christ—toward sanctification, and ultimately, glorification. To thrive on this path you need to resolve the issue of your salvation, to settle it. The journey is difficult enough as it is without the extra anxiety of continually wondering where you stand, checking spiritual Facebook first thing every morning to see if your relationship status with God has changed overnight.

Let me say it again: Peace with God is not a feeling; it is a fact. You don't lose it when you stumble, and nobody can take it away from you. Unlike us, God is not fickle in His relationships. If you are in Christ, your sins have already been dealt with once and for all. It is already true and established in the heavens. The task before you now is simply to live in light of that fact.

## Chapter 8

# ADAM AND ME

Therefore, just as sin came into the world through one man, and death through sin, and so death spread to all men because all sinned.

—ROMANS 5:12

**W**HY DO PEOPLE die?"

"Why is there disease and sickness?"

"Why does it seem that life, at its core, is broken?"

"Why is there natural disaster, famine, terrorism, and war?"

"If God is good, why does He let so many good people suffer?"

"If God really loves me, why has He not taken this pain away?"

More simply put, just "Why?" It is the question at the dead center of human existence in all its complexity and pain. If you have lived long enough, you've asked it. If you have ever lost someone you loved to tragedy, or gotten a terrible diagnosis yourself, it's a question that has haunted you late at night. It is the question we grapple with over and over in a world that, despite so much beauty, goodness, and wonder, is terribly wracked with all kinds of suffering.

Romans 5:12 is one of the most significant verses in the New Testament, precisely because this is where Paul answers this lingering *why* question: "Therefore, just as sin came into the world through one man, and death through sin, and so death spread to all men because all sinned." For Paul, historically and theologically, the story comes back to *one man*.

Through the tale of two men, Adam and Jesus, Paul sums up the entire story of the human species in all its heartbreak, comedy, and loss. All the living and all the dying, all the pain and loss and joy and wonder fits into this master story. The story of these two men tells the story of us all. To understand the beauty and power of Jesus' story, we have to understand Adam's story first. Without the agony and grief of the first half there is no way to access the delirious joy of the second half.

## SIN ENTERED THE WORLD
## THROUGH ONE MAN

Adam's story starts in the Garden of Eden—a garden created by God, a perfect, triune being who is not just loving but is Love itself. God was not lonely, bored, or insecure—there was an unbroken circle of reciprocal delight between Father, Son, and Spirit. Out of that goodness, out of that abundance of love and joy, God created us. It was for no other reason than to enjoy Him and be enjoyed by Him. That was what life in the Garden of Eden was about, and that was *all* it was about.

The primal story, the origin, began in wonder and innocence. Everything was green, lush, and beautiful. There were no cities, and there was no smog, no hustle and bustle. There were no tears—only a perfect world not yet corrupted by pain. There was no fear, and there was no death. All there was in the beginning was a man and a woman. They loved each other, and they loved their God. They wore no clothes because they knew no shame.

Adam and Eve had the world itself as their playground. There were animals to name, and there was intimacy to enjoy. They walked leisurely through undomesticated fields yet untouched by the terror of the night. The world was a buffet of light and color, and they ate and drank freely of everything they desired. They were unfettered, unburdened—they were, in every sense of the word, wild and *free*.

None of us has been to this place, and yet we long for a world unspoiled, a world without death or chaos. On some level we know that is the kind of world we were made for, not a world of violence, sickness, and decay.

Adam and Eve needed nothing; they lacked nothing.

Anything and everything in this glorious new creation, where every blade of grass and every clear stream was radiant with God Himself, was theirs for the taking. They could eat and drink as much as they wanted, and they feasted on the love they shared with their Creator and with each other. Nothing was off limits—nothing, that is, except for one tree.

The fields and trees were bursting with fruit and berries created for them to enjoy. God told them that the only tree they were not to eat from was the tree of the knowledge of good and evil. Note it was not an "evil tree"—everything in the garden was created good, like the God who created it. It wasn't a "bad tree"; it was the tree that brought the knowledge of good and bad, right and wrong. In a word, it was the tree of *judgment*. They didn't need judgment, because they lived lives of easy dependence and perfect trust. Judgment was God's job, not theirs, and there was no reason to try to assume God's role because God provided everything they needed. The tree represented the limits of their human existence; it was the place where they were supposed to acknowledge God as God.

But one day the serpent slivered up to Eve in the garden and began whispering in her ear. The words he slithered so softly are words we all know and recognize: "Did God really say that? Did God really tell you not to eat of the tree? Did He tell you that you would die? You would surely not die!" (See Genesis 3:1–4.) You've heard that voice, too—the voice that says, "Surely He didn't really mean that!"

Before that moment Adam and Eve had not doubted the goodness of the Creator for a millisecond. But now the idea crawled through Eve's brain like a worm. "For God knows that when you eat of it your eyes will be opened, and you will be like God, knowing good and evil" (Gen. 3:5).

It was the very first experience of FOMO (fear of missing out). Evidently the fear of missing out started all the way back in the garden, even before we could see pictures of other people's exotic vacations on Instagram! Curiosity suddenly seized Eve. What would it be like, she wondered, to *really know the way God knows?* What would it be like to see the way only God can see? The world she inhabited was perfect; she needed nothing else. But she looked at the fruit, and it appealed to her yet-innocent eyes. It seemed succulent and delicious. *How could one little bite be so bad?* Eve was overcome by the desire to know the unknowable. She gave the fruit to Adam, and he ate with her.

On one level it all seems so odd and counterintuitive—to eat of the only tree from which you are forbidden to eat! But on the other hand, if you are reflective on your own life and journey at all, you know *precisely* how and why this is possible. It's true even of the most innocent child—you want nothing more than the thing you cannot have.

Could the story have gone any other way, given our collective human FOMO? We don't know. What we do know is that Adam and Eve's story has become the human story—that we are a people never quite satisfied with what we've got, even when what we've got is enough. We are a people fatally attracted to a little bit more, willing to give up all the good we've got for what little bit we don't have. It is the human instinct every gambler knows all too well.

And just like that, everything changed. Suddenly Adam and Eve felt the bitter taste of shame in their throats—they knew they were naked. For the first time they knew what it was to want to hide. Eden itself may have been no different yet, but they saw it all differently and experienced it all differently. Because at that moment, as Paul wrote in Romans 5:12, "sin came into the world."

The contagion was released. Sin invaded human DNA. Sin was now loose in the earth, and there would be no going back. Now the virus affects us all, which is the doctrine of original sin. It is not just that we commit individual acts of sin, but that we are born sinners—sin is passed down to us through Adam, just as eyes and ears and noses were passed down. In this way we all bear the likeness of our ancestral father. Like Adam and Eve we are still very much created in the image of God, which is why we have a capacity for love, creativity, and wonder. But in the DNA of Adam, we have the same proclivity toward sin.

Sin entered the world through just one man.

## DEATH ENTERED THE WORLD THROUGH SIN

Have you ever made the long, lonely walk to an open casket, seen the face of someone you loved now with no color in their cheeks (save some makeup from the mortician), looked at the shell of that beautiful person now no longer animated by life and spirit—*and felt OK about it?* Of course you haven't. No matter how long a person has lived or how good a life they have lived, death always feels unnatural somehow. Death always feels like an interruption.

Death was not God's idea. Death was not part of God's original design. God's intentions for humanity were only for life, life, and more life. Death was not part of God's program—death was a penalty. Death was the consequence of our insistence to do it our own way, to attempt to play God rather than to trust God. Instead of living from dependence and trust, Adam and Eve tried to become self-sufficient, and we are all living out the implications of that choice even now. Now death comes to us all, and there are no exceptions.

We are now all subject to *physical death*—you could say that from the moment of birth we all begin to die. Every step forward in life is one step closer to the grave. And it is not just physical death that reigns in us, but *spiritual death*—separation between God and us, that perfect communion severed. Now we all know what it is to be fractured and fragmented; we know what it is not to feel whole and connected, at peace with one another and with God. The death that sin ushered into the human species does not wait until we breathe our last to plague us; we feel its grip even now in the enmity, racism, and division we experience in the world. Even that is not the full extent of the reign of death—now there is also *eternal death*, separation from the living God that goes on forever in a place Jesus describes as the place of outer darkness.

Paul makes the provocative claim that it wasn't just Adam and Eve who sinned, but all of us: "Therefore, just as sin came into the world through one man, and death through sin, and so death spread to all men because all sinned" (Rom. 5:12). It is not just that we all now have a sin nature—though that is true—nor is it that we will all do something specifically sinful—though if we live long enough, that is true too.

We were just a twinkle in his eye...but we were there. We were bound up in him, and our story was somehow intrinsically bound up in his story. Like a member of Congress acts on our behalf and represents us, Adam served as the representative of the entire human species. What happened to him happened to each of us.

Now every person is born into sin. Now every person is born into death and is already dying.

## THE HUMAN STORY: TAKE TWO

It is bleak to consider all the ways that sin and death come to reign in an entire species as the consequence of one man's sin. And there has been so much horror, pain, and dying ever since. Human history is an endless laundry list of plagues, wars, and calamities, a cycle that continues even now.

Thousands of years later, though, a glitch came into a story plagued by death and decay. Another man came—not into a garden, but into a stable that smelled of animal excrement. He didn't grow up in the wonder of paradise but in a world where even during His infancy His family had to run from the terror of a homicidal king.

When He was fully grown, the same dark presence that slithered up to Eve in the garden slithered up to Him in a desert. His lips were cracked, and His skin was weathered from the elements. His ribs jutted out obtrusively as symptoms of starvation began to show.

Satan had thousands of years to work on his presentation—and keep in mind, it had already worked the first time! He came again to sow seeds of doubt about the good intentions of the Creator. He came again looking for some tiny nook or cranny of human pride to exploit, to offer the comforts of a life fit for a king to a solitary starving man from Nazareth, a man now battered by the desert winds.

Three times he made his offer, with the world itself on a platter for the tired and hungry Son of God. All the weight of human history thus far had gone the way of Adam and Adam's sin. Once again the fate of the world hung in the balance, and once again the accuser brought his full array of charms to bear.

The emaciated man listened. Unlike Adam and Eve, He had not been enjoying the splendor of the garden but was worn down by the searing heat of the desert sun and the relentless cold of the desert nights.

There was no tree in the desert, but really, the same fruit was being offered all over again. But this time something remarkable happened.

His bones were weary and His body weak, but His eyes were clear. This time, the man didn't flinch. This time, *the man resisted*.

And the world would never be the same.

## FIND YOURSELF A WHOLE NEW STORY

The Genesis story shows us that we live in a fallen world that is not yet in accordance with God's perfect will. It was never God's intention for us to suffer—in fact, it breaks the heart of God to see us suffer. A world of chaos, violence, and pain is the legacy of Adam, and none of us is untouched by it. God loves us too much to override human freedom and autonomy, so in love He lets us have what we chose.

But this is not the end of the story. If sin spread like a contagion into all humankind through the sin of Adam, how much more so does the antidote of grace spread through those who are now in Christ, the second Adam? The story of Jesus is not a sequel to the story of Adam—it's a reboot! The creation story is being retold, and it isn't a story of death, decay, and pain—it's a story in which all things connected to that old order are passing away and all things are being made new.

If you are tired of the constant heartache that goes along with inheriting the story of Adam, there is good news—now you can choose to find yourself in a whole new story!

*Chapter 9*

# IN CHRIST

We were buried therefore with him by baptism into death, in order that, just as Christ was raised from the dead by the glory of the Father, we too might walk in newness of life.

—ROMANS 6:4

WHEN I WAS in my early teens, our family visited the Grand Canyon. The vibrant colors coupled with the sheer size of the canyon made an indelible impression on my fourteen-year-old mind. I remember looking at it and thinking it was like a real-life, gigantic postcard. When I returned years later to white water raft the canyon, I was reminded again of the grandeur of the canyon and the magnificent colors and rock formations. I returned from that trip telling Debbie that she needed to experience it for herself. So in the fall of 2017, when Debbie and I took an extended season of rest in Sedona, we took a day trip to the Grand Canyon.

As we entered Grand Canyon National Park, I wondered if the canyon would live up to the hype and if seeing it for the first time would strike her as deeply as it did me. We parked the car and began walking the path to the scenic overlook, the quintessential, iconic view of the canyon from the South Rim. All of a sudden Debbie began to jump like a kid at Christmas while tears welled up in her eyes. Then with hands lifted high she began to worship the only One capable of making such an incredibly majestic scene.

In the same way, when you come to Romans and grasp what God has done in saving us, it has that same kind of dazzling, breathtaking effect. Grace surprises us, changes us, and then, as we begin to grasp its grandeur, overwhelms us. Now we merely see "through a glass darkly," to use Paul's phrase, and still the wonder of grace can be almost too much to take in. Only in heaven will we truly appreciate the magnitude of what God has done. Surely we will, in the words of the hymn "Amazing Grace," feel that "when we've been there ten thousand years," we will have just begun!

But even if we do not have the cosmic view to take in the full beauty of God's plan, it is vital that we behold it—savor it, think on it, meditate on it—to the fullest extent that we can. We still see plenty of things in this world and ourselves that are not yet right, and each of us has more than our fair share of flaws, struggles, and insufficiencies. But in every situation that is less than God's ideal and less than we would desire, there is grace; grace that not only covers our sin but also permeates our lives and produces spiritual life in us.

The idea is not that you need to get your life together so you can have a better grasp on what God has already accomplished for you in Christ. Rather, getting a clearer, crisper, sharper vision of what God has already done for you in Christ is the only way you will be able to get your life together! When we get to Romans 6, Paul paints a vivid word portrait of grace, in all her vibrant colors, precisely so we can open our eyes, behold, and marvel.

We still find ourselves in the middle of an ancient war between light and darkness, good and evil. We still find ourselves in the grit and grime of real life, with its ceaseless stream of challenges, conflicts, and temptation. We are offered a glimpse of the beauty of grace not to distract us from the fight, but because only this beauty will carry us in the midst of such things! To see what God has done and is doing for us in Christ changes our perspective on everything and everyone else and allows us to see the battle from a higher point of view.

## STRATEGIES FOR OVERCOMING SIN

No matter how much we might grasp the beauty of grace, we are always tempted to forget. From the first time I saw the Grand Canyon to the next, there was a lot of life in between. We have plenty of words, images, noises, and competing distractions that would attempt to crowd out an aerial view of grace.

So when we find ourselves pulled back into the battle with sin, the first and most crucial strategy is not always easy to do, but it is profoundly simple: we are called to *remember*. To remember what? To remember that we are justified; to remember that God has forgiven all of our sins—past, present, and future; to remember that God has removed our transgressions as far as the east is from the west. We are no longer wearing the tattered robes of our own righteousness, which Isaiah said are "as filthy rags"; we are clothed in the righteousness of God. All of this happened the moment we first placed our trust in Christ—a faith that did not originate within us; even faith itself is a gift of grace!

Because we are now in Christ, Jesus' story has become our story. Our individual stories are chock full of pain and death. But according to Romans 6:3, we are now baptized into Christ's death—not water baptism, but a way of saying all of our sins, sorrows, and suffering have been swept up into His death and are buried along with Him.

But because Christ was "raised from the dead by the glory of the Father [by the power of the Father], we too might walk in newness of life. For if we have been united with him in a death like his, we shall certainly be united with him in a resurrection like his" (Rom. 6:4–5). In other words, what happened to Christ has now happened to us. When we followed His descent into the grave, we too were swept up in the inevitability of resurrection.

His story is now our story. It is not up to us to engineer

some kind of victory over a foe Christ has already defeated. Instead we remember His story over and over again. We recall it. We rehearse it. We read Scripture to remind us of His story; we sing songs about His cross and resurrection; we call it to remembrance—or better yet, we ask the Holy Spirit to bring His story to our remembrance throughout the day. The battle with sin has already been won, and we now share in His tremendous victory. As His death became our death, His triumph has now become our triumph.

On the cross Jesus uttered, "It is finished." The heavy lifting was done for us when the weight of the entire world was placed upon His lacerated shoulders. He carried the weight we could not carry. And now that we have shared in His crucifixion, Paul writes in 2 Corinthians 5:17 (NKJV) that "old things have passed away; behold, all things have become new." You look in the mirror to see the same eyes staring back, but the resurrection power of Christ now surges within you.

For Paul this is not an image or metaphor—it is the rock-hard truth of things. You can only die once. And if you have died with Christ, the old you is dead and gone—forever! The new you is all that remains. This is not sunny optimism, the power of positive thinking, or seeing the glass as half-full instead of half-empty. The old man or woman is dead and buried with Christ, and a new creation is all that we are now, as we have been united with Him.

The point here for Paul is that we are dead to sin, alive with Christ, and now have power over the forces that once held us in bondage. Sin no longer has dominion over us. But to avoid giving people a license or excuse to sin, many Christian movements throughout history have mitigated the extent of this good (best!) news. Some of us who came up through some version of the holiness movement were convinced that every time we fell short, God would abandon us, causing us to question our salvation every time we sinned.

The truth is, when we do fall into sin, it does not negate the reality that we have already been justified in Christ—it is rather only a symptom that we have forgotten the deepest truth about ourselves. The task then is not to start all over in our life with God but to remember the truth of what God has already declared to be true about us. In our guilt we start to believe old lies about ourselves, lies that have already been shattered by resurrection power. We rehearse old narratives, playing back reels of old tapes of blame and accusation instead of rehearsing the story of God in Christ.

Instead of remembering, we are tempted all the more to forget. In our shame and condemnation we feel as if we are somehow now separated from the One who loved us and gave Himself for us. But those feelings are far from facts; those feelings are lies. Our sin does not alienate us—God has already dealt with our sin once and for all, through the death and resurrection of Jesus!

You have already been forgiven. When you fall, God doesn't kick you out of the house and leave you to your own devices. God does discipline us, to be sure, because according to Hebrews 12, a good father disciplines his sons. But discipline is not abandonment. It is only a manifestation of God's relentless love. He simply loves us too much to allow us to get stuck in the same old cycles and patterns forever, so grace pulls us forward.

But God's love doesn't let up for a moment. In our worst moments of shame God tells us He loves us way too much to let us go. Like any good parent, God doesn't isolate or abandon us when we fall—He showers us with more attention, not less! That sense of estrangement in our minds can be powerful, brutal. But it is an illusion. For those who are in Christ, our stumbling does not equal separation.

If you are struggling with some habitual sin (a "besetting sin," in the language of Hebrews), this is not a reason to hide from God but a reason to lean in all the more. God can use even our struggles as a way to draw us close to Himself, making us less dependent on ourselves and more dependent on Him and His grace.

## CONSIDER THIS

Because the sense of separation exists only in our minds, and Christ has already accomplished His victory over sin, death, and the grave, our minds are actually the only battlefield that remains. It is why Paul will tell us later in Romans to "renew our minds." Here in Romans 6, after rehearsing the story of Christ's victory for us again, he tells us to "reckon [ourselves] to be dead indeed to sin" (v. 11, NKJV). In other words—*consider it and hold it before you.* Consider yourself dead to sin. We are to think of ourselves as dead to sin because God says we already are! When we remind ourselves of this, we are not claiming a promise but accepting a fact.

Remember this. Replay it. Rehearse it. Revisit it. Read Romans 6 every day of your life if you need to, because it will always ground you in the reality, in the truth of what already is. If you fill your mind with this truth over and over—saturate yourself with this truth, marinate in it—your body will follow.

No wonder, then, it is not until after Paul tells us to reckon ourselves dead to sin that he instructs, "do not present your members to sin as instruments" (your hands, your feet, your eyes, your ears, your mouth), but rather "present yourselves to God" (v. 13). We do not present our members to sin—because we legally cannot present them to sin! God already owns us, has already bought us with a price through the death of the Son. Now our lives are not our own. We don't have to click our heels together three times, hope really hard, and try to make it so. We merely have to align ourselves with the truth of what God has already said and done!

As we remind ourselves of this truth, we slowly start to give sin less opportunity. Instead of lingering on websites that you know are not healthy for you, remaining in conversation with someone who is not your spouse, or allowing rage to run wild in you, simply give yourself to God. You offer up your body as "a living sacrifice, holy and acceptable to God" (Rom. 12:1), not because you are compelled to, but as a natural, free response to the love God has poured out on you through Christ Jesus. Now you live for Christ's pleasure; you live to bring Him glory! In everything you say and do, you want your very life to articulate your thanks for who He is and all He has done.

You do not live under the bondage of sin anymore. You do not "let sin reign in your mortal body," because you are literally outside the jurisdiction of sin. You have crossed the borderline from the dominion of sin into the freedom field of grace. Sin simply has no authority over you now, no rights to you, no claims on you. You are God's now—all God's and only God's. Remind yourself of this over and over.

Paul is telling us, *This is already done, so go ahead and live this way!*

## Chapter 10

# DEAD TO SIN

What then are we to say? Should we continue in sin in order that grace may abound? By no means! How can we who died to sin go on living in it?

—ROMANS 6:1–2, NRSV

**D**EBBIE AND I were both only nineteen years old when we got married in Wisconsin. I had just finished up my sophomore year at Central Bible College. We had moved back to Colorado to work for the summer, and we were living in a house that actually used to be a chicken coop! But we were young, we were newlyweds, and being able to live together was way more important than where we lived! The more pressing problem was that we needed to move back to Springfield, but we had no idea where we were going to live or what kind of jobs we could get. When I think of our lack of planning and preparation, I still can't believe her parents let us get married!

Every day we would pray and ask God to open doors for us—for a place to live and a place to work. One day, out of the blue, I got a call from a funeral home in Springfield. The owner told me he'd heard I was going to be a junior in college and that I was recently married. He wondered if I would want to work at the funeral home. He said we could live in the funeral home rent-free and they would pay me a salary with the understanding that I'd be going to school during the day and then work for them on afternoons and evenings.

To be sure, working in a funeral home was not something that had even entered my mind. If you are a funeral director, the Lord bless you—but I said I'd need a little time to think about it. The owner said he couldn't hold the job for long, but that he was willing to give me three days. I got off the phone and told Debbie about the job offer. She asked me, "Well, what did you say?"

"I told him I'd have to think about it."

"Um, what is there to think about? We need a place to live,

you need a job, and now we'll have both. I mean, come on. It's all right there. What is there to think about?"

"Well now wait a minute," I said. "You're not going to be the one doing it...I will!"

We proceeded to have a little discussion about what it would actually mean to work at a funeral home. In a comic bit of poetic justice, the first night we lived there, about midnight, I got my first call. A person had passed away, and I was to accompany one of the funeral directors to the morgue. That meant Debbie would be alone in the mortuary. And business just then was, shall we say, very good! There were six individuals who just weren't very talkative!

Any of us who have been around for a while have probably lived in closer proximity to death than we are comfortable with. But in Romans 6, Paul begins to talk about death in a whole different way—not the terror of death that has reigned through Adam, which we read about in Romans 5, but a way of being "dead to sin." Paul explains that those who have been justified and made alive in Christ are actually *dead to dying*...no longer subject to the death that has reigned through sin. Because all of our own death has been absorbed, even swallowed up, into the death of Christ Himself, we are now also sharing in the power of His resurrection!

Death came to us all through just one guy. But in the same way that death reigned through the death of Adam, death's antidote now reigns through us.

## SO...WHY NOT KEEP ON SINNING?

Romans 6 is easily one of the most important passages in the New Testament, but it is also one of the most easily misunderstood. That's because people commonly read it as if Paul is changing the subject from everything in chapter 5. But he isn't; it is very much an expansion of the same idea. After Romans 3–4 explained that the first step in salvation was justification, Romans 5 explained that all of us live under the reign of either sin or grace. He argues that in the same way that when Adam sinned, we all sinned, the reign of Christ inaugurated in the death and resurrection of Christ is now just as pervasive as Adam's sin ever was. In fact, grace is even more pervasive! Whereas sin dominated our lives before, grace now pervades us even more than sin did. Whereas the reign of Adam colored everything with death, the reign of Christ now colors everything with life.

As under the reign of sin it was inevitable that we would all ultimately die, now it is inevitable that all who are in Christ will conquer death. The salvation that God has begun in us, He will be faithful to bring to completion! Grace is more than a one-time gift or something that God "did." Paul presents grace as an active force, a demonstration of God's power continually at work in us in the present, in the midst of all our trials and struggles—grace is what God is doing right here, right now, the power at work in all who are saved!

Paul's vivid portrait of life in Christ under the reign of grace is even more hopeful than the reign of death through Adam was discouraging. If so much pain, suffering, and violence could come through one man's disobedience, how much more does life—abundant, belly-bursting life!—now come through the obedience of the Son of God Himself? It is an intoxicating vision, a whole different way of seeing the world. In Christ truly *everything* has changed!

By the time Paul gets to Romans 6, he can imagine the person hearing this letter read aloud in a small, early Roman congregation asking the question, "Well, wait...if all my sins are forgiven—past, present, and future—and God already views me as righteous...then I guess it doesn't really matter how I live, does it?" He anticipated the same question that people raise now whenever the grace of God is preached in all its reckless beauty: "Well, why not just keep on sinning, then?"

Some preachers are still scared to death of this question, so afraid of giving people a license to sin that they neuter the gospel of grace and preach a watered-down gospel—one that places greater emphasis on individual responsibility than it does on God's majestic plan and work of grace. The problem with that approach is that it minimizes God's work in us all the while fostering a works righteousness that makes salvation more about us and less about God. But note that even for Paul, if grace is preached rightly, in all its force and power, the question that will inevitably be raised is, Does it matter how I live? The truth is, if people aren't raising that same question now when they hear the gospel proclaimed, the gospel has not yet been rightly proclaimed!

Paul's response to his own rhetorical question is emphatic: "By no means!" Or, "God forbid!" In other words: "That's *crazy*! It's unthinkable!" His reasoning here is fascinating, and the language is provocative to this day: When we were in sin, we were dead. But now that we are in Christ, we are actually dead—to sin itself! The reign of sin simply has no power over those of us who are now under the reign of grace; we are simply no longer under sin's sway. We have been drinking from the river of God and are now intoxicated with grace—we are *under the influence*!

# WHEN CHRIST'S STORY HAS
# BECOME YOUR STORY

It is a powerful image, to be sure—dead to sin, alive to Christ! But it still leaves the nagging question of "How, exactly?" If you are reading this, you are still here. You have not experienced death and have certainly not been hanged on any crosses. How in fact did we die to sin? Consider Paul's gorgeous reply in Romans 6:3: "Do you not know that all of us who have been baptized into Christ Jesus were baptized into his death?"

Water baptism is an important sacrament for Christians, a powerful outward sign of an inward grace; a potent reenactment of what God has done for us in Christ. But water baptism is not what Paul has in mind here. Rather, the idea is that we have been baptized "into Christ Jesus" Himself.

In other words, His story has become my story. His death has become my death. All of our loss, our heartache, our sin and addiction and shame—all of it has been crucified with Christ on the cross. It doesn't matter whether or not you "feel" it. It is not something that you now need to achieve or do. It has already happened! When Christ died to sin, we died to sin. While He never sinned Himself, He entered the human realm, which is a realm of sin, and His death severed our relationship with sin entirely. When He was "finished" dealing with sin, we were finished with sin, too! When He was buried, we were buried along with Him, and all our sin and pain were taken into the abyss, never to rule over us again.

The really exciting part is this: since His story has become our story and His death has become our death, His resurrection has now become our resurrection. As He died, we died. As He was raised, we are now raised. Everything that happened to Christ has now happened in us and through us. We are forever dead to the reign of sin and now live only under the reign of grace. As Paul declares in Romans 8:11, the same power that raised Jesus Himself from the dead is now at work in us.

And it never stops. Twenty-four hours a day, seven days a week, grace is always humming, always moving, always working. Even while we are asleep, grace is still affecting us, shaping us, changing us, directing us, preparing us, strengthening us, and even disciplining us, though that is not our favorite part to think about!

It was inevitable when the Son of God was laid into the ground and "descended into hell" (in the language of the Apostles' Creed) that He would come up out of the ground in power and victory. As you have now shared in His death, that same ultimate, final resurrection is inevitable for you too. Nothing will stop the healing power at work that courses through you even now—absolutely nothing. No one can stop it. Your story is not over, but the outcome is already certain. The only inevitability now is that resurrection, not death, will have the last word over you. As Paul writes in Philippians 1:6 (NLT), "And I am certain that God, who began the good work within you, will continue his work until it is finally finished on the day when Christ Jesus returns."

Why will you not continue to live under the domination of sin? Because Christ has already accomplished the victory, and His victory has become your victory.

## Chapter 11

# THE FRUIT OF RIGHTEOUSNESS

But now that you have been set free from sin and have become slaves of God, the benefit you reap leads to holiness, and the result is eternal life.

—ROMANS 6:22, NIV

**W**HEN MICAH WAS eight years old, his dad pastored a small but thriving church in southern Missouri—until the day came that he was arrested for embezzlement. Overnight his entire life changed. Instead of attending weekly church services, Micah and his mom attended weekly court proceedings. Ultimately his dad went to prison.

Micah remembers going there for the first time, his dad walking out of the back room in a jumpsuit with tears streaming down his face. He wasn't even allowed to hug his son. But he knelt down and whispered, "I'm so sorry I failed you." He felt as if he had failed not only his son but also his God.

Nothing was the same for Micah after that. His dad had been a superhero to him. If his dad felt as though he couldn't measure up, Micah figured there was no way that he could either. His family stopped attending church. While his dad eventually got out of prison, he was still on the run from God. Micah absorbed his father's sense of inadequacy in anything pertaining to the things of God. He felt less than other Christians and hated them for it.

When he got to high school, Micah had some freedom. He was able to branch out from his house for the first time, and within months he was drinking, smoking, and doing drugs. He fought with his parents, too—if he couldn't keep God's rules, he saw no point in trying to keep theirs. It all got progressively worse until, finally, Micah's dad asked him to leave the house. At sixteen, he was homeless.

Micah moved in with his girlfriend, and at age seventeen they found out she was pregnant. "I was already a failure to God," he thought to himself, "now I've really sealed the deal." Having sex before marriage seemed bad enough to him; having a child out of wedlock was a whole different matter. The guilt pushed him even further away from God. The day before he walked across the stage to receive his high school diploma, his girlfriend gave birth to their first child. Overnight he went from being a kid who played in a band and rode a skateboard to being a father.

While most fathers would greet their new child with joy, Micah felt only terror. He saw in his son's little face a visceral reminder that he really didn't have anything to give; he was empty, broke, and still just a kid himself. But that crushing weight motivated him to do more and be more. He got a good job in sales, making more money than many of his friends' parents at only nineteen years old. He started finding success but still felt *so empty.*

Around the same time his girlfriend started attending James River Church and had an encounter with Jesus that changed her life. She suddenly wanted to get baptized, serve in the church, and stop having sex until they were married. Micah felt threatened. For him it was the same old story of the church stealing his happiness again. When they fought, he would tell her all the reasons church, Christians, and God were bad. But deep down the nagging truth was that he felt *he was bad* and that she had joined a club he couldn't be a part of. The more he felt left behind, the more the emptiness grew.

One night in the heat of a fight things got bad enough that she decided she needed to leave. "Fine!" he said. "Go! I can get any girl I want." But his life continued to spiral downward. He wasn't happy. He found himself constantly retracing the trajectory of his life, thinking about how much better it could have been if he had not made so many mistakes.

He kept up the appearance of success with his friends, but the interior of his life was in shambles.

Then one day he decided that being apart from his girlfriend and son was what was making him so unhappy and decided he was going to win them back. In a grand gesture he went out and bought the biggest diamond ring he could afford. He asked her out to dinner and planned the proposal. When the night came around, he got down on one knee, opened the box, but before he could even get the question out, she told him no. *What?*

Her faith had become vital to her. She told him she didn't want to be with someone who didn't love God. Out of desperation he agreed to go to church—even though the church had become the sum of all his fears. He just knew everyone would know he was a sinner when he walked in the door. After spending years working hard to prove he was as good as or better than anyone else, he was back in the one space that made him feel inadequate.

He stood straight as a pencil during the worship, surveying the congregation, watching out of the corner of his eye while people worshipped. He didn't exactly hate it, but he didn't really feel anything either—until the message started. Micah listened to the sermon about how God had loved him and planned for his salvation before time began, how He sent Jesus to die for him, and how Jesus was calling to him now. He heard that Jesus would cover him in His own righteousness so he could stand blameless before God, no matter what he had done. "And I've done an awful lot of things," Micah thought. He was caught off guard. He was unnerved, and yet he felt as if he was on the verge of stepping into some unimaginable freedom. It was as if the entire case he had built against God and the church all shattered at that moment.

Micah gave his life to Christ that day. And for the first time he felt free—free from sin, free from guilt, free from shame, and free from his own accusations. He married his girlfriend a few months later. They got involved serving in the church, and his whole life began to change.

The church people he had once feared and spoken bitterly about loved him and made him feel as if he'd found a family. They answered his questions and walked with him as he battled his issues. Strangely, the more Micah began to discover the love of God, the more he found he didn't even want to do the same things anymore—because he was beginning to love God, too. The feeling of emptiness he had tried to fill with drugs, sex, money, and success was finally filled in the way that only God could.

Micah had seen all too clearly the ways that his sin had affected everyone around him. But the more he began to understand grace, he realized it worked the same way—it changed everyone around him, too! Two years ago his dad came with him to James River Church and rededicated his life to Christ. Coming to understand grace changed him into a completely different person. A year later his sister-in-law came to church, and Micah saw grace change her, too. A few months later his mother-in-law came with them, became a Christian herself, and finally came clean after years of addiction to drugs and alcohol.

Micah's story dramatically illustrates the difference between the wages of sin and the fruit of righteousness. In his former life not only did he have to reap the natural consequences of his own actions, but even when he tried to get his life together, all the weight landed on him. It was work, all work, his work...lonely, alienating, soul-wearying. But when he heard the message of grace, he was able to open up his hands instead of clenching his fists. He stopped trying to prove or earn anything, and in return everything was given freely to him as a gift.

And if the wages of sin affected the community of people around him—see how much more the gift of God transformed all the people that he loved! That is the beauty of grace: for however much damage the wages of sin may bring to our lives, the fruit of righteousness is far more bountiful than anything we wrought under the curse of sin.

## THE WAGES OF SIN

As Micah's story demonstrates, we are always presented with two different choices, two wildly divergent paths. Bob Dylan wrote a song about the fact that we all serve either the devil or God, and he was right.

Depending on which master we choose to serve, two different sets of benefits and two different destinies are offered to us. The results of our choices are as disparate as the masters these choices represent.

No matter what path we choose, we *are* going to be mastered. Sin is a master, and God is a master. But they are radically different. This dichotomy between two different masters and the two kinds of life they offer runs through every human being: all people are either justified or not, living under grace or living under wrath. There are no exceptions. Paul makes a simple but profound distinction between how these two masters exercise rule over us: *sin pays wages; God gives gifts.*

We are all familiar with the concept of wages; it is the language of earning, debt, and obligation. You make an agreement with an employer to take a job, who commits to compensate you for your time and pay you a certain amount of money. So long as you do the work, the owner or company is indebted to pay you the wage you rightly deserve. The proof of this is that if they did not pay you, you could take them to court; they are legally obligated to pay you what you earn.

The world apart from God is a world of wages—of getting what you earn, getting what you deserve, and nothing more. Instead of grace, without God we are left with some version of karma: what goes around comes around. The trouble is that, as we've already established that we are all sinners, "the wages of sin is death" (Rom. 6:23). Even at our best we have all missed the mark; we've all fallen far short of what we were intended to be. This is why in the end the world's system of earning and wages never works out well for us—because in the final analysis, the only logical wage of sin, the natural end of sin, is always death.

Note that the language of sin, then, is that of wages—of work! At first this might seem strange because sometimes when we sin, it doesn't feel like a sin at all. Scripture is frank in telling us, that sin is, in fact, pleasurable for a season. For fleeting moments sin feels like fun—sin feels like freedom. We are able to do whatever we want and act on whatever we feel whenever we feel it. What could be freer than that?

The trouble is, sin is deceptive. Like our work, sin wears us down, sin wears us out. But it's a very different wage than the life-giving sense of purpose that good work can bring us. Over time sin depletes us and dehumanizes us. Every choice we make that bends toward self instead of God and our neighbor diminishes our humanity. Our life, our vitality, and our wholeness slowly decrease. Our greed diminishes our capacity for contentment. Our lust diminishes our ability to have healthy relationships. The further we go into sin, the more the juice of life slowly dries up. There is no rest, no peace—no *shalom*, in the Jewish phrase—no wholeness, and no sense of well-being in our souls.

The wages of sin are relentless. We reap what we sow. This reality of wages, of sowing and reaping, is an endless, inescapable hamster wheel of cause and effect. We never actually make progress; we never actually go anywhere. The wheel keeps turning—the only thing that changes is that we get more and more depleted and exhausted.

The wages of sin ultimately separate us from God—not only in this life but also in the world to come. The natural end to such a life is hell, which Jesus describes as a place of outer darkness (Matt. 22:13). It is dark because God is light. Hell is a realm where the light of life and love is completely gone. In the absence of God all we are left with is pitch-black darkness—left with literally nothing. There is no joy, no passion, and no meaning. And this abyss just goes on and on forever, leaving people with nothing but pain and regret.

## THE GIFTS OF GOD

In the final analysis, the end result of a life lived only in the world of wages is bleak indeed. But in contrast to this economy of sowing and reaping, of getting what you deserve, God offers a radical alternative: the economy of grace—an economy based on gifts!

Everybody knows the joy and wonder of a gift, the wide-eyed joy and innocence of a child unwrapping presents on Christmas morning—a little boy or girl who hasn't done anything to earn these things, lost in the joy of opening one gift after another. The only thing more intense than the delight they feel in opening their presents is the giddy delight of the parents who give them. And we all know the unique joy of a gift that is unexpected, that seems to come out of nowhere—a gift we could not have anticipated because it is beyond our reckoning or imagining.

Whereas a life apart from God is all wages, a life with God is all a gift, a complete gift, *and nothing but a gift*! In contrast to the wages of sin, which is death, the gift of God is eternal, unending, everlasting life. Salvation really is the gift that keeps on giving, that just keeps unfolding throughout eternity. It starts here and now, in this present moment. As Jesus tells us in the Gospels, he who believes on Him has "already passed from death into life" (John 5:24, NLT).

The moment we come to faith in Christ, He begins undoing the damage of sin; He begins making us new. He actively chose us before time—"I want him, I want her, I want him…I want her!" He chose us to be part of His family. Like the prodigal son who comes home and is immediately given his father's ring and robe and sandals, followed by a lavish party—from the moment we first come home, God lavishes His love upon us. But it's only the beginning. God's plan, God design all along is to give His sons and daughters gifts throughout eternity.

In heaven everything is new, and all things are being made new all the time. It is human nature to like new things—a new house, a new car, a new phone, a new job. There's something about that sensation of having something brand-new, something that has never been used before. This is what the realm of heaven is like all the time. The idea is not that we just sit around playing harps all day for eternity; rather, every moment is full of surprises. God is always giving gifts. It's how He rolls!

## SANCTIFICATION

The more Paul's beautiful vision of salvation unfolds, the more radical and comprehensive it becomes. It is staggering in its depth and scope. Salvation is not simply a matter of praying some one-off prayer, securing some kind of eternal fire insurance, and going on with your life as it was before—it's a whole new way of being in the world! What God has done for us in Christ changes everything. It will change everything for you, just as it did for Micah.

But even after people have an experience with Christ, so many of us still struggle with the assurance of this great salvation. How can we know that this magnificent work has been or is being done in us? According to Romans 6:22 (NIV), "But now that you have been set free from sin and have become slaves of God, the benefit you reap leads to holiness, and the result is eternal life." Simply put, if you have been genuinely saved, the by-product is holiness. As Jesus Himself taught so clearly in the Gospels, the fruit of a life with God is different from the fruit of a life lived only for self. If we are truly in Christ, the natural result of our union with Him is sanctification.

If we don't have the fruit of holiness in our lives, if over time we are not becoming more like Christ, then our lives are clearly not yet rooted in God—not yet rooted in love.

The fruit of loving God is sanctification that culminates in eternal life. If the end of sanctification is eternal life, then without sanctification there is no eternal life, and thus we could only conclude that we have not yet been truly saved. Martin Luther taught long ago, "There is no justification without sanctification, no forgiveness without renewal of life, no real faith from which the fruits of new obedience do not grow."[1]

The word might sound dense and theological, but really it is full of beauty, simplicity, and freedom. To sanctify is to set apart, to consecrate for a special purpose. To be saved is to be set apart for a truly stunning purpose: to be completely remade until we are fully formed in the image of Christ Himself. Sanctified people are not perfect people; they are growing people. Slowly, gradually, and sometimes incrementally we are growing in grace, growing in Christ.

Ultimately sanctification is nothing less than falling deeper in love. Think about what happens when someone falls in love—the way caring for someone else completely reshapes their desires and reorders their priorities. People who are in love do all kinds of things they ordinarily wouldn't do, things that wouldn't come "naturally" in the life they lived before, because they are now living to please their beloved.

When John Wesley talked about sanctification, he described it as being "made perfect in love."[2] The idea was some kind of moralistic perfection—not about sinlessness but about complete, wholehearted devotion. The idea is that the more the love of God is perfected in us on the inside, the more our behaviors on the outside start to align with the heart of God. Our affections are being changed, and our desires are being conformed to Christ's desires for us.

It doesn't mean we are no longer tempted to sin, but it does mean our appetites are gradually being transformed. Some of the things that used to taste good to us don't taste so good anymore, and we find ourselves craving God where before we only craved our own pleasure. Everything about us may not be righteous yet, but we "hunger and thirst for righteousness," to quote Jesus (Matt. 5:6), and so we will be filled!

That's exactly what Micah described in saying that after he came to Christ, he started to sense his deepest desires shifting as he began to fall more in love with God. Early on he still struggled with the assurance of his own salvation. But as I told him in my office one day, that is often just the enemy trying to confuse us as to where we stand with God and make us feel unsure. Satan will accuse us and try to get us to doubt our salvation. That is why we have to remind ourselves of our justification constantly, regardless of whether or not we feel it! The more we trust that and live as if it is the deepest truth about us—even when emotions come and go—the more we will see our outward lives begin to change and be reordered.

Thus, in a life with God, the focus of all spiritual practices—when we pray, read Scripture, worship—is always interior change, heart change. Our behavior is not perfect yet (certainly not in the sense of there being no room for improvement!), but our hearts are perfectly His. As we grow to love God more, God is actually perfecting us, in that He is fitting us together for our intended use. Whereas before our desires were fractured and fragmented and we erratically chased whatever made us feel good or feel loved, grasping manically for a sense of identity, the love of God makes us whole. That is what sanctification looks like: holiness is really all about wholeness!

## Chapter 12

# RULES-BASED CHRISTIANITY AND OTHER OXYMORONS

In the same way, my friends, you have died to the law through the body of Christ, so that you may belong to another, to him who has been raised from the dead in order that we may bear fruit for God.

—ROMANS 7:4, NRSV

WHEN DEBBIE AND I got married, in many ways I was still a bit of a punk. For the most part I was young in my faith, and while I had changed, when it came to acting and thinking like Jesus, I had a long way to go! A few days after our wedding we were making our way across South Dakota en route to exotic Rapid City, hardly the honeymoon capital of the world.

As stone age as this might sound to some of my younger readers, we didn't have GPS or Siri; we were on our own. We had planned to stop by a mall to pick up some things we needed before heading into the Black Hills. Suddenly I realized I had missed the exit. Seeing a median crossing about a quarter mile up the road, I made plans to cross it and head back in the other direction. Debbie, raised a pastor's daughter, was taught to play by the rules and saw the world in black and white. Immediately she spoke up: "John! You can't do that."

"Sure I can…It's no big deal," I said.

"John! You really cannot. Look—the sign says 'authorized vehicles only.'"

"Debbie! We live in a country with a government of the people, by the people, and for the people. I'm one of the people…and I'm authorizing myself!" (Like I said, I was still a bit of a punk!)

My statement of self-government was followed by what can only be described as deafening silence. Once I parked the car, Debbie jumped out, walked into the mall, and left me sitting in the food court for the next hour and a half. As I sat there alone on my honeymoon, I realized I had a long way to go! At that point in my life it was like a Marriage 101 course on what *not* to do as a husband. Since then I've become less careless and more thoughtful both with my words and in my actions. The longer I live with Debbie, the more I love her and understand her.

As we do life together, I'm not following some kind of rule book. Instead, after all these years there are things that I know please her and things that disappoint her. Because she is my very best friend, I would never want to intentionally offend or hurt her. It doesn't come out of a sense of duty or obligation; there is no drudgery to it. When you really love someone, it brings you joy when you can bring them joy. For example, Debbie loves fresh flowers, so most weeks I buy her flowers. It brings a smile to her face, but more importantly it is a regular reminder of how much I love her. And the fruit of living that way over the long haul is that we have the kind of relationship where we can finish each other's sentences. One of us might sing a line of a song, and the other will say, "I was just thinking about that song in my mind." That's the kind of oneness that comes naturally, intuitively, from living to please each other.

In a very real sense that's how following Jesus was intended to work. It's not supposed to be about obligation and ritual. It's a love story! Paul writes of the relationship between Christ and the church as a marriage. As with any healthy husband and wife, love calls us to get lost in serving and caring for each other. There is safety within the commitment of this relationship, so you don't have to live in perpetual fear that if you say or do something disappointing, the other person is going to walk away. Rather, "love covers a multitude of sins" (1 Pet. 4:8). This is precisely what it means to live under grace.

## WANDERING BACK INTO
## THE LAND OF THE LAW

The trouble is, we always end up wandering back into the land of the law. In Romans 5–6, that's the contrast Paul has been drawing: between living under the law or living under grace. The law can be understood either as the Ten Commandments, the Pentateuch (the first five books of the Bible), or the law of God written on our hearts. Broadly speaking, the law speaks to whatever a person knows they should or shouldn't do. So long as you view keeping the law as a means of salvation—or a way to achieve right standing with God—you have stopped walking in grace and have placed yourself back under the law.

Now the truth is, almost nobody who has been in a relationship with God or in church for a significant matter of time would articulate their faith that way. People will often at least make some sort of token, lip-service acknowledgment to the role of grace. People may have heard that in justification, all their sins are forgiven, and they begin a new life in Christ.

But here is the reality that often plays out in real life: A person comes to saving faith in Christ. Then someone comes along, congratulates him on becoming a Christian, and tells him some things that will really help him grow in his relationship with Christ. She explains that prayer is a way of talking to Jesus and encourages the new believer to spend a few minutes each day communing with God. There's certainly nothing wrong with that! And then she says, "Here's a new Bible," and tells him it's God's love letter to him and it will help him. There's nothing *wrong* and, in fact, everything *right* with these classic spiritual practices.

But from there the list begins to grow. "Be sure you attend church regularly. Go to a class on spiritual growth. Join a weekly Bible study. Start giving in the offering. Get new friends to help you stay on track. Start volunteering regularly in your church and in the community. Oh, and there's a list of things you need to avoid: don't gamble, don't cuss, don't drink, don't think bad thoughts, don't tell dirty jokes, don't gossip, don't watch certain TV shows or movies..."

Now, with the list complete and the person sufficiently loaded down with dos and don'ts, we tell him to go enjoy his freedom in Christ, and wonder why he begins to believe his relationship with God is contingent on his personal performance.

The problem is not that any of these disciplines or encouragements are bad. They can be a huge source of strength! The trouble is that we can inadvertently, in the words of my friend Larry Osbourne, "make the *tools* for discipleship the *rules* for discipleship." All of the things that were meant to foster relationship with Christ become the yardstick for measuring how well we are doing at pleasing God. And questions intended to promote spiritual growth become the catalyst for condemnation.

"Did you pray today?"

"Well, I meant to, but actually, I overslept."

"Did you read your Bible?"

"Well, I read a couple of proverbs, and it was pretty helpful...but I probably really should be doing more than that."

"How often are you in church?"

"Well, I missed last Sunday. I know I should be more consistent."

Then, when you do make it to church, you have a fight on the way, so you don't feel like singing, and suddenly God feels distant. You have a bad day and find yourself using some of your old vocabulary in traffic, so you berate yourself for being a terrible Christian.

Supposedly you were saved by grace, but now you are beginning to gauge your standing with God based on how well you keep the rules. Your efforts become the metric for evaluating whether God is pleased with you. You find yourself wallowing in guilt for not performing well enough or long enough.

There are moments of spiritual warmth, where you feel as if your heart is right with God again. But inevitably that slide, that constant condemnation, plays out over and over again, discouraging you, wearing you down. It's the reason so many people end up giving up on church altogether—they become exhausted by trying to keep all the rules. And because they can't keep the rules, tragically some give up on their faith altogether.

## THE STRUGGLE IS REAL

This common struggle is what makes Romans 7 so important. It is where people often lose sight of the extraordinary grace message of the entire book and get lost in the proverbial weeds. It can feel like a detour from the broader movement of the texts—Paul going from celebrating the remarkable work God has done for us in Christ to the violent inward struggle of Romans 7, climaxing with "O wretched man that I am! Who will deliver me from this body of death?" (v. 24, NKJV).

There are endless debates about Romans 7—whether this

struggle is Paul's own or that of a theoretical person; whether this struggle describes life before salvation in Christ or after salvation. Over the course of my life I have preached it both directions myself! But in the debate over the context and details of Romans 7, we lose the focus of this brilliant chapter entirely. Whose struggle the text describes, and where in life such a struggle occurs, is simply not the point.

Romans 7 is perhaps the most profound analysis of sin in all of Scripture. It gives us keen insight into the psychology of sin, the nature of sin; how sin interacts with the law of God, and whether that law is written on our hearts or written in the Bible.

Prior to coming to Christ every person is under the law— and as we saw in chapter 4, they will be judged by the law. In that sense all of humanity is linked to the law. That is the basis for what Paul writes at the start of Romans 7. In Paul's analogy in Romans 7, at one time we were bound to the law the way a man and woman are bound together in marriage. But the marriage covenant, powerful as it is, only binds until one of the parties dies. We were once married to the law, Paul says. But now that we have come to faith in Christ, we are dead to the law. How did that happen? When Jesus died on cross, He took the punishment the law prescribed as the penalty for our sin. When He died for our sin, He died to the law. And since we are in Christ, when He died to the law, we died to the law.

Part of the good news of grace is that we are dead to the law! Because Christ through His death satisfied the demands of the law, the law has no demand on Him. Since we are in Christ, when He died, we died with Him. And like Him, in the eyes of the law we are dead. Now stay with me for just a minute, because this is a very liberating truth. In the law's eyes it is as if I am dead, which means I am completely outside the jurisdiction of the law and the law cannot condemn or accuse me.

Paul's point in Romans 7 is that before we came to Christ, we were under the law. We were married to the law. And it wasn't a very happy marriage. The law was continually saying, "Do this, don't do that, you didn't quite do this right, you keep messing up in this area of your life." But since we were saved, we are no longer married to the law; we are married to Christ. We are in a love relationship with Him, and our goal is to honor and please Him.

When Christians forget this reality, invariably they default to living as though they were once again married to the law. In reality it's like a woman who was widowed from her first husband but then remarried only to live with her new husband as if he were her first husband. Pretty weird, huh? And yet Christians do it all the time when they don't understand grace and don't walk in grace. Instead of living as if they are married to Jesus and pleasing Him, they live as if they were married to the law and live to please the law. And the result is a rules-based Christianity that is devoid of grace and dependent on personal achievement.

When we wander back under the law, it constantly fosters feelings of personal condemnation because we are never able to measure up to the law in our own efforts, no matter how hard we try. The joy of our salvation is diminished because we feel as if our salvation is up to us, again. And ultimately, rules-based Christianity will outright rob you of your joy.

But if instead we have died to sin in Christ, we are resurrected in Him and live to serve Him. This is not because we *have* to—we *get* to! It would be like a preacher telling a groom at the end of the wedding sermon, "Now you have to kiss the bride." You don't *have* to kiss—you *get* to kiss! This is about love, not law! Romans 7:6 (NLT) declares that now in Christ "we can serve God, not in the old way of obeying the letter of the law, but in the new way of living in the Spirit."

Because we now live as people married to Christ, constantly feeling His delight in us as sons and daughters of God, we naturally live to please Him. It comes from a place of joy and adoration. Yes, the description of life under the law is dire; rules-based Christianity is lifeless, limp, and joyless. But if we understand just how oppressive the existence described in Romans 7 really is, we can understand why it reaches such a stunning crescendo in the first verse of Romans 8: "There is therefore now no condemnation for those who are in Christ Jesus"!

Rightly understood, seeing the truth of that verse is like watching a million fireworks go off just in front of your eyes. But whether this ends with a bang or a whimper, whether it makes you shout or yawn, whether that declaration invokes a golf clap or a shout depends entirely on how you read Romans 7. You can't fully celebrate the radical nature of this hope unless you understand the hope first.

## Chapter 13

# THE FRUSTRATION OF TRYING TO PLEASE GOD ON MY OWN

I was once alive apart from the law, but when the commandment came, sin revived and I died, and the very commandment that promised life proved to be death to me. For sin, seizing an opportunity in the commandment, deceived me and through it killed me.

—ROMANS 7:9–11, NRSV

**D**ETERMINATION CAN GET you into trouble. When I turned fifty, I hit that phase of life when you start to come to terms with not being young, but there's still that part of you that wonders if you can turn the clock back. Deep down I wondered if it was possible to get back in the kind of shape I was in when I was in my twenties. Around that time there was a boot camp type of fitness class that had started meeting at James River, and the people in it kept asking me to join. Eventually I gave in and decided, *I'm going to do this thing.*

All my life it has been my style to attack anything I do head-on. So when I went to that first class, I tackled it with the same kind of enthusiasm and grit I always had. Who cares about being fifty? And as advertised, boot camp put me through the gauntlet: push-ups and sit-ups, mountain climbers, bear crawls, floor sweepers, squats, and a lot of running in between. In typical Lindell style I went after it as hard as I could. I've always been competitive, and I've got enough pride not to let myself be outworked! It was exhausting, of course, but when it was all said and done, I felt pretty good. "I'm not thirty anymore, but I've still got it"—or so I thought.

Later that day Debbie and I headed out of town to celebrate our anniversary. We enjoyed a beautiful dinner by the river and afterwards decided to take an evening stroll along the promenade. That's about the time it hit me—my quads were on fire. My hamstrings were so tight that you could've played the "Orange Blossom Special" on them! As we came to some steps, I realized that my legs were so sore, I needed to take the wheelchair ramp just to get to the top. All the while I was thinking "How am I going to get onto the platform to preach on Sunday?"

Ultimately nothing was bruised except my ego. It wasn't a big deal. But in microcosm it's an image of how many Christians end up trying to take on a life of holiness. We grit our teeth, clench our fists, and determine we are going to get it right this time—no matter what it takes. But instead of getting stronger and faster, we only get more exhausted, overextending ourselves until we can barely move.

## HOW SIN SEIZES AND DECEIVES

The law, in and of itself, is good. It shows us what a righteous life looks like and sets borders and parameters for our lives. But the law, for all of its intrinsic good, does not have the power to save us. It can tell us what to do, but it cannot empower us to get it done. Neither does it have the ability to transform us. It shows us how far off we are from hitting the mark, and in the words of Romans 3, shows us just how true it is that "all have sinned and fall short of the glory of God" (v. 23). Worse yet, even when we know the law, we can't keep it.

In Romans 7 Paul makes a fascinating statement: while the law in and of itself is good, sin actually tries to use the law against us! It makes sense when we consider that all the enemy ever really does is distort and pervert the very things God intended for good. There is nothing Satan is not willing to try to use against us.

According to Paul, the law is actually the mechanism God uses to reveal sin to us. It tells us what things are sin, to be sure, as we see in the Ten Commandments. But there is also a deeper kind of "knowing" of sin that the law makes possible. Romans 7:7–8 (NRSV) says, "If it had not been for the law, I would not have known sin. I would not have known what it is to covet if the law had not said, 'You shall not covet.' But sin, seizing an opportunity in the commandment, produced in me all kinds of covetousness." That second kind of knowing implies a firsthand knowledge, an experiential knowledge. In the Garden of Eden, Adam "knew" Eve. They made love; they experienced each other. In a similar manner, this is not head knowledge but lived experience—like "knowing" what it is to touch a hot stove and be burned!

Intrinsically our human nature makes us want to have something the moment we are told we cannot have it. Anybody who has ever raised a child knows this is true on an almost primal level! The moment we are given a concrete limit, our hearts are inclined to test it.

A hotel on Padre Island, Texas, sat right on the water. Given the proximity, the owners knew people would inevitably try to fish from the hotel balcony. So they put up signs everywhere that said, "No fishing from the hotel balcony." Sure enough, within days you could see fishing lines coming from all over the hotel balcony; everybody was fishing. Finally they took the signs down—and people stopped fishing from the balconies of the hotel! It's human nature.

You could paraphrase verse 8 this way: "But sin, creating a base of operations out of the commandment, produced in me all kinds of covetousness." This is why a rules-based approach to godliness will inevitably fail us every time. Law, as opposed to love, doesn't actually motivate us to keep the law of God, but to break it!

Paul takes this a step further in Romans 7:11 (NRSV) when he claims, "For sin, seizing an opportunity in the commandment, deceived me and through it killed me." Sin can deceive us; it can use the law deceitfully in all directions. It can deceive us about righteousness—causing people to think too highly of themselves on the one hand and to condemn themselves on the other hand. Either method is equally effective because so long as righteousness is based on our own performance, we lose either way—whether through hubris or indulgence.

Sin can also deceive us into thinking the law is unreasonable, as if God is a cosmic killjoy trying to keep us from having fun. This is especially unfortunate because what we see in Scripture over and over again is a God relentlessly committed to human flourishing. In Jesus we have a God whose stated goal for us is that we "may have life and have it abundantly" (John 10:10).

God has created so much for us to enjoy. The truth is, sin diminishes our humanity in a way that numbs our senses to joy and beauty. That is part of the deceitfulness of sin. The nuances of ways sin can deceive us seem endless. Sin can fool us into thinking God is against us, or just make itself appear more attractive!

If this feels redundant or repetitive, there is a reason I want to thunder it home: because Paul did. Because he was "a Hebrew of Hebrews; in regard to the law, a Pharisee" (Phil. 3:5, NIV), he knew all too well how the law could be commandeered for sinful purposes. In his former life he actually killed Christians in the name of keeping the law! So he was ever vigilant and aware of the ways the law itself could actually be used to keep us away from God and from God's purposes for our lives.

## BACK TO LOVE

Without wanting to overstate the case, the choices couldn't be starker: we will go either the way of the law or the way of love. And sadly, without love the law that reveals and provokes sin in us won't do us any better in the grand scheme of things than lawlessness does.

Anybody who ever attempts to follow the law—even just to be a "good," moral person—has the same experience: it turns out to be a self-defeating experience. Our good just isn't good enough. And no matter how valiantly or vigorously we attempt to keep the commandments in our own strength, it always ends like my first day at boot camp—we are so exhausted from trying to get it done in our efforts that we give out and are unable to move forward.

In the last chapter I talked about my struggles early in marriage to figure out how to please my partner—how that has become a lifelong pursuit, born not of obligation, but of delight. As a pastor one of the things I love about serving the same church for many years is seeing how people learn to love at different ages and stages of life. More recently I've been inspired by the way some couples I've known have loved each other in their twilight years. It has been beautiful to watch.

The generation in their eighties and nineties now had different roles and responsibilities during their prime earning years than those we have now. In their generation it was more common for the man to go off to work and the woman to take care of the house while he was away. So it was really moving to see, when an elderly woman in our church was physically failing, the tenderness with which her aged husband cared for her. He had his own health problems to contend with, but he was right there by her bedside at the hospital. The doctors told him that she would be going home soon and he would need to be physically strong to care for her: "You have to get your own rest," they said. But he couldn't leave her, for no other reason than that he wanted to be there. Even as one night became two nights, and two nights became three nights, and three nights became four...he could not bear to leave her side.

When you see that kind of love, what you see is not the strength of a vow. That kind of commitment is not about mechanically trying to keep your word, just for the sake of words that were spoken long ago. There was something much, much deeper that motivated him. He was there not because it was a matter of law but of love. Love fulfills the law—you end up there because you want to be there and choose to be there. The secret to the Christian life is not to master the rules but to fall more deeply in love. The rule of law, however hopeful it might seem from afar, ultimately cannot liberate us. In fact, it is the very thing Christ came to liberate us from!

## Chapter 14

# NO CONDEMNATION

There is therefore now no condemnation for those who are in Christ Jesus. For the law of the Spirit of life has set you free in Christ Jesus from the law of sin and of death.

—Romans 8:1–2

I HAVE CLIMBED A few actual mountains in my time, but nothing I've ever done compares to Mount Rainier. An active volcano, Mount Rainier ascends to an astonishing 14,410 feet above sea level and stands as the true icon of an already stunning Washington landscape. When I was on sabbatical a couple of years ago, I decided on a whim that I wanted to climb it. Debbie traveled with me so she could spend time with her sister, who lives in nearby Seattle, while a friend and I were going to climb.

The night before my adventure, Debbie and I went out for a nice meal. While sitting at the table, she said, "You know, John, you haven't even looked up anything about this climb yet. Don't you think it would be a good idea to do at least a little research before you go in the morning?" Having grown up in Colorado, I had done a fair amount of hiking at high altitude, so honestly it hadn't crossed my mind to read about the climb.

Sitting at the table, I leisurely googled to find out what I could about climbing Rainier for the first time. As I perused blogs from people who had actually climbed it before, my eyes widened and my stomach tightened. I moved quickly from "this is going to be fun" to "maybe I should have given this a little more thought." As I lay awake that night, replaying all the harrowing descriptions I had read a few hours before, I hoped I hadn't lost my mind in signing up for a trip I had not bothered to read about.

As we got ready to climb the next morning, the outfitter who helped us prepare didn't say anything to alleviate my concerns. He was quick to remind us that some people had died on the mountain and that the trip had an inherent danger which would necessitate each climber signing a waiver. The next day was spent roped in groups of four trudging around in the snow so we could practice using our ice axe in the event of a fall. Our instructor dutifully told us, "Pay attention to everything I am teaching. Your lives depend on knowing what to do if this happens."

The first day we hiked to 10,500 feet, ate some supper, and were sent to bed by 7:30 p.m.—the final ascent would begin at 1:00 a.m. that night so we could traverse the ice fields while the ice was still frozen. It is a thrilling thing to cross a crevasse that is several hundred feet deep in the dark! I was tied to the three people ahead of me as we began the ascent up the aptly named Disappointment Cleaver. I had an ice axe in my left hand, with what appeared to be a several-hundred-foot drop to the right—the path no more than eighteen inches wide in some places. All I could see was what was in direct view of that tiny headlamp.

For the last hour and a half we slowly made our way up to the summit, encountering sixty-mile-per-hour winds and blowing snow that stung our faces. There was more than one moment when I wondered, "Why am I doing this?" I imagined at my funeral somebody saying, "Well, at least he died doing what he loved," and I thought to myself, "But I don't love this *that* much!"

As treacherous as it was, getting to the top was nothing short of euphoric. As every climber knows, the view from the top along with the sheer exhilaration of making the climb provide a feeling and perspective that few things in life can match.

Mountain climbing seems almost designed for metaphor. I can't help but think that many of our lives feel that way. We start off having no idea what we've gotten ourselves into, what the journey is going to mean, or what it will require of us. I believe a life of faith especially feels that way—we say yes to Jesus because the message of the gospel speaks to the deepest longings of the human heart. But saying yes to Him is much like saying "I do" in marriage. How could Debbie or I have known what those two little words were going to mean when we spoke them in front of family and friends at nineteen years old? You can't see where the journey will take you; you just know it's a journey you have to make. And so you trust.

In this way the journey Paul has taken us on thus far in Romans very much mirrors the human journey. Paul has taken us into the valley, into the deep crevasses of sin, through the treacherous lows of our existence. We've climbed through the controlling power of legalism and seen how even the good law of God cannot bring the freedom our souls so desperately desire.

And then in Romans 8:1 we reach the top. This is where it was always going, the pinnacle of Paul's thought and argument and the high peak of human existence. You've made it this far, both in your own treacherous journey and through this walk on the Romans road. Don't rush past this too quickly. Lay down your gear, breathe deep, open your eyes, and let yourself take in the view from the top as these words wash over you even now: "There is therefore now no condemnation for those who are in Christ Jesus."

But knowing these words are the summit, knowing the grandeur they possess and the magnificence they hold doesn't automatically mean this truth becomes your new reality. Most Christians understand these words are powerful, but not every Christian experiences their power. So where is the disconnect? Why is it that we can sing about it, celebrate it, study it, and still struggle to actually live it?

## NO MEANS NO!

The trouble is that for all our familiarity with Paul's words, most of us have never really grasped the gravity of what he is saying. Because the gospel rightly understood is always better news than we could have ever dared to imagine, there seems to be a subtle amendment Christians make when they read these words. Paul says *"No* condemnation," but we read it as *"Less* condemnation." As in, "There is therefore now *less condemnation* to those who are in Christ Jesus..." And do you know what? Most of us tend to carry around an awful lot of condemnation if we are honest; less condemnation would actually be pretty good news! But this is not pretty good news, not even just good news—this is *the best* news!

Paul isn't talking about something that comes later. He isn't talking about heaven after you die. He isn't talking about when you get your act together, or when you are on your death bed. He's talking about real life, right where you are, *right now*. It happened the millisecond you first got saved, and it extends into this exact second. There is not and there will never be any condemnation for those who are in Christ Jesus.

*"No* condemnation." It is definitive and without qualification. Have you ever given a *really hard* no? As in, "No, I will not go on a date with your cousin Ralph." As in absolutely not, most certainly not, of course not, under no circumstances, by no means, not at all, negative, never, nope, nada, huh-uh, nah, not on your life, no way Jose, ixnay... *never*.

Hear this in the depths of your soul: the Christian is a

person who has been taken completely out of the realm of any possible or conceivable condemnation. The Christian has literally nothing to do with condemnation. There is no condemnation now, and there never *can* be! It is actually impossible for the Christian to be in a state of condemnation in her relationship with God. It simply cannot happen!

Because this is objectively true for those in Christ, you should never allow yourself to feel condemnation. Don't let the devil make you feel it. And if he does, stand up and say these words right back to him: "There is therefore now no condemnation for those who are in Christ Jesus!" Let Scripture be your response to every lie and accusation, and he will flee from you.

If you have given your life to Christ, you are no longer a son or daughter of Adam. You are not *in* him—you are not *in* sin. Those who are joined *with* Christ are now *in* Christ. You don't move in and out of Christ based on how you feel from one moment to the next, even based on what you do from one moment to the next! It's not about what you feel; it's about what you know.

## BUT WHAT ABOUT WHEN I SIN?

This sounds so good, but can the good news really be that good? Why is it that when we hear the words of Romans 8:1, we struggle to actually believe that this truth is the definitive word on our relationship with God? Perhaps the problem is that we are better acquainted with our own brokenness than we are with God's goodness. You know the reality of your own heart and life. You have a ringside seat to see the darkness of your own sin. So how can there be no condemnation when you are all too aware of your own imperfection?

Here's the thing: being in Christ doesn't mean that you will never sin again. But what you have to understand is that when you do sin, you are no longer sinning against the law—you're sinning against love. For a non-Christian, that is not true. Revelation talks about the book where all our deeds are recorded, good and bad, to be judged. It's like someone sinning against the laws of the state of Missouri; if you sin against the state, you are at the mercy of the state. The state gets to determine both the crime and the punishment. But the law (of the land) has no jurisdiction over a dead person. Our relationship to the law has been severed. It simply does not exist.

If we sin now, we sin against love. It would be like a husband or wife who has done something to offend their spouse. Of course it wouldn't be something they would want to do, because it causes pain to their spouse. We never intentionally cause pain to the people we love. Within a marriage our actions can, in fact, break someone's heart, but they don't break the law. The marriage commitment and trust bear up under the offense. When you cause hurt, you apologize and try to do it right next time.

Romans 8.2 declares, "For the law of the Spirit has set you free in Christ Jesus from the law of sin and death." Note this is in the past tense—*has*. It has already occurred, in your justification. When you were justified, God accomplished for you that which the law could not. God accomplished for you what you could not! This is the truth that has to reframe everything about the way we see the Christian life, including how we look at ourselves and how much we look at ourselves.

The trouble with much of contemporary Christianity is that we spend far too much time and energy in spiritual self-assessment, making everything in our life with God about us—how we feel, what we think, an endless preoccupation with "I." But in the words of Scottish pastor Robert Murray McCheyne, "For every look at yourself, take ten looks at Christ."[1] To really live in the power of "no condemnation," we have to keep our eyes on the person who makes that possible—and that's not you. It was never your perfection; it was always His. It was never your action; it was always His. It was never your righteousness; it was always His! That's why it is so critical that you keep your eyes on Him. Our "performance," like our feelings, will wax and wane. There will be good days and bad days, but the basis for our confidence is only found in Christ.

## OUR GREAT TEMPTATION

In Christ we are those who, in the words of Romans 8:4, "walk not according to the flesh but according to the Spirit." Walking in the flesh is often taken to imply some kind of gross sin. And sure, those of us who are now in Christ, because of our deep love for Him, would not casually live a life of indulging in things that we know break His heart. But I don't think that is what Paul primarily has in view here. "Walking in the flesh" does not by any means necessitate living an overtly sinful life. Rather, it calls to mind the words of the apostle Paul in Galatians 3:3, "Are you so foolish? Having begun by the Spirit, are you now being perfected by the flesh?"

In Paul's time this was the great temptation for the early Christians. False teachers would come through and tell them, "Yes, you have been saved, but now you have to go and do these things." And those who had come to Christ by a gift of sheer grace were pressured to attempt to sustain their status with God by going back under the law; thus, those who had already been set free could live as though they were in bondage.

I am convinced that is still our great temptation: to take our eyes off Jesus and the spectacular work He has accomplished for us and in us through His death and resurrection, and to put the attention back on ourselves—*our* work, *our* spiritual disciplines, *our* prayer life, *our* holiness, and *our* willpower.

But we were not intended to live that way—we weren't set free from slavery just so we could go right back into bondage! Rather, it is now the Spirit of God that works in and through us to love God and to please God. It is not about our efforts. It is not about the strength or voracity of our will or our commitment. It is not about steeling ourselves by sheer force and deciding to hold on. It's freedom! It's freedom from the weight of condemnation. It's freedom that enables us to keep our focus on Jesus. It's freedom to rely solely on what has been done for us rather than anything from us!

It is not up to us to win any battles. Our whole goal, our only goal, is to *surrender.*

## Chapter 15

# A NEW WAY OF LOOKING AT THINGS

You, however, are not in the flesh but in the Spirit, if in fact the Spirit of God dwells in you.

—ROMANS 8:9

ROMANS 8 is not only a crown jewel of the Book of Romans, but also of the Bible itself. The Presbyterian pastor Donald Grey Barnhouse once asked twenty pastors what chapter of the Bible they would choose if they could have only one chapter with them on a desert island. Five of them chose Romans 8. The more of this glorious text we come to see, the more we understand why. It is bookended by two powerful words at the beginning and the end: "no condemnation," and "no separation." What could be better news than that?

In this chapter we find out that all of God—Father, Son, and Holy Spirit—has been conspiring all along for your salvation. God the Father, the judge, justifies us. Jesus, the Son, intercedes for us; like a lawyer, He advocates and pleads our case. And the Spirit of God comes alongside us, "helping us in our weakness," praying for us and through us.

In contrast to the image of Jesus as our advocate, Satan is described throughout Scripture as the "accuser of the brethren." All of our lives we have stared down accusation. Some of it has come from this enemy of our souls, some of it has come from people around us, and much of it has come from our own selves, looking in the mirror. We have heard the well-rehearsed charges against us many times—all the bad things that we are, all the good we have not lived up to, all the ways we stumble and fall short.

But when we come to the court of heaven, we find out the case has been rigged—in our favor! It's as if you were pulled over in a small town and went to a trial where your father was the judge, your elder brother was the defense attorney, and the jury was made up of your family and friends. The enemy conspired against you, but he could not outscheme

God's triune conspiracy of hope. God wanted you and chose you from the beginning, and nothing could get in the way of Him getting you back!

But while all of God has been working on your behalf right from the start, there is a marked shift in emphasis in the role of the Trinity in Romans 8. Up until this point the Holy Spirit has been mentioned only one time. In Romans 8 alone, the Spirit is referenced twenty times! For all the ways we've seen that life with God differs from life under the law, it is really the Spirit that makes all the difference.

Where many of us have understood our salvation in ego-centric terms—it's all *I, I, I*, about my effort, my resolve, my feelings, my commitment, my work—God's plan was for His own Holy Spirit to do all the heavy lifting. It doesn't mean there isn't a role for you to play. But it does mean that your salvation is not contingent on you, your effort, or your work. Rather, life with God is really all about cooperating with the Spirit, yielding to the Spirit, allowing the very essence and power of God—the same power that raised Jesus from the dead!—to work in you, through you, and for you.

The moment you become a Christian, the Holy Spirit actually begins living and dwelling inside of you. In 1 Corinthians, Paul says "you are the temple" of the Holy Spirit—you are the sanctuary, the holy place where God now lives. But this reality of becoming a dwelling place for the Spirit begins the moment you are saved.

In Romans 8 we see that the Spirit works powerfully in us. God's Spirit is not just at work in you when you are doing overtly spiritual things—when you are reading your Bible, fasting, praying, or worshipping. The Spirit is at work in you continually—even while you sleep! When you groggily first begin to wake up, long before your morning coffee, the Spirit has already been hard at work on your behalf. The Spirit never lets up or lets off, never takes a nap or a vacation.

## THE WORK OF THE SPIRIT

And what is this work that so preoccupies the Spirit all day every day? To help you, to strengthen you, to bring you along...to *change you*. Ultimately, to conform you to the image of Christ Himself until everything in you and about you is shaped in the likeness of Jesus. The Spirit is empowering you to live for God, to love God, and to know God. The Spirit is revealing the heart of God, the words of God, and the will of God to you, leading and directing you in the paths you are to take.

We've spent a lot of time looking at the work of God in your salvation because that is the foundation on which everything else about a life of faith is built—so it's terribly important to get the foundation right. But the work of the Spirit is not *only* about salvation, and certainly is a lot more comprehensive than the forgiveness of sins! The Holy Spirit empowers you, in the real world, in your real life, to accomplish God's work in the world right where you live.

There have been so many times in my life when I've been in desperate situations that I simply cannot imagine being able to have resolved on my own—moments when I've felt surrounded, unqualified, overwhelmed, and have seen no way out.

When I was twenty-two years old, and Debbie and I had a six-month-old baby, I became the pastor of a rural church. The church had developed a reputation for being a kind of wild bull no pastor could ride for long. The previous two pastors had short, troubled tenures. And within my first few weeks in the role there were no indications my time was going to end any differently. We faced a seemingly endless flood of calamity. On my first day a boy in the church shot his younger brother in a tragic accident. My second week I had to sit through a guest speaker the church had already booked who was a clear charlatan—using Jesus' name to coax people into giving him Cadillacs and jewelry, telling "miracle" stories that turned out to not be true. But I was the young, green rookie pastor who had no credibility yet, and I knew it wasn't my place to say anything.

Financially the church was in dire straits. Within the first eight weeks the vice-chairman of the board came to tell me they were unilaterally cutting my salary by 25 percent because they were behind on their payments for the building and had taken out a loan for back pay they owed the previous pastor. So the weight of that financial strain landed squarely on my shoulders too.

Maybe all the logistical challenges wouldn't be quite so bad if I won everybody over with my winsome personality and youthful, newly minted pastor charisma, or had the management savvy to put together a dream team of leaders. But let me put it this way: within my first few months one board member resigned and another board member threatened to beat me up. And another board member took me out for a drive one day to inform me that he had not voted for me and didn't think I would make it as pastor there.

I was young, naïve, inexperienced, and in over my head. There was no conceivable reason to expect a rookie pastor would be able to turn around a church in nowhere, Kansas, under crushing debt with a dysfunctional leadership culture. But precisely because I knew I was not qualified and the situation seemed impossible to navigate, I was desperate for God to move. I leaned hard on the Holy Spirit because I knew I didn't have the answers myself—and miraculously, grace took over. The Spirit began to move in ways that can't be accounted for by any human formula. Within a year we paid off all the church's debt, attendance more than doubled, and we started seeing new people come to faith in Christ every week!

It reminds me of Acts 11:23 when Barnabas arrived in Antioch and rejoiced. When the grace of God is realized in a place or in a person, it's going to be life altering. By the time we left that church, we had become so attached to the people that it took us a year and a half to get over having to say goodbye to them. That wasn't my work—that was the work of the Holy Spirit giving us supernatural grace!

## THE WAY OF THE FLESH

While Romans 8 describes the limitless promise of life in the Spirit, Paul also contrasts it with another path—life in the flesh. As always, God is relentlessly committed to human freedom, and we do get to choose. Note the contrast:

> Those who live according to the flesh have their minds set on what the flesh desires; but those who live in accordance with the Spirit have their minds set on what the Spirit desires. The mind governed by the flesh is death, but the mind governed by the Spirit is life and peace. The mind governed by the flesh is hostile to God; it does not submit to God's law, nor can it do so. Those who are in the realm of the flesh cannot please God. You, however, are not in the realm of the flesh but are in the realm of the Spirit, if indeed the Spirit

of God lives in you. And if anyone does not have the Spirit of Christ, they do not belong to Christ. But if Christ is in you, then even though your body is subject to death because of sin, the Spirit gives life because of righteousness. And if the Spirit of him who raised Jesus from the dead is living in you, he who raised Christ from the dead will also give life to your mortal bodies because of his Spirit who lives in you.

—ROMANS 8:5–11, NIV

We will be governed either by the Spirit or by our own fractured desires. Either we will go the way of the flesh, which is hostile to God's law, or we will submit to the Spirit, who shapes our lives in a manner that is pleasing to God. There is no middle ground here.

It is important to be clear on what Paul was *not* saying— his use of the word *flesh* here has been terribly misunderstood in ways that could not have been fathomable to him or his early readers. Some people have interpreted these words to mean our bodies themselves are somehow inherently bad— as if all God cares about is that which is spiritual as opposed to that which is tangible and real. It is easy to develop a high-minded Christianity that is abstract and disconnected from the earth, about ideas and ideals instead of the grit and grime of life in our bodies.

But this could not be further from what Paul had in mind. In fact, he spent a considerable amount of time and energy in most of his letters combating the prevailing philosophy of his day, gnosticism, which is the notion that all that is bodily or earthly is evil and everything spiritual is good. Gnostics, then and now, believe that "salvation" is about transcending your body and your bodily existence. In contrast, Christianity could not be more bodily.

God is revealed to us in bodily form through the man Christ Jesus—that is what we call the incarnation. Everywhere Jesus went, He touched blind men and lepers, spit in the mud to heal a man's eyes, and healed a woman with an issue of blood who simply brushed up against the hem of His garment. The body of Jesus was torn and mangled on the cross; the body of Jesus was physically resurrected from the dead! And early Christians held on to the promise that what happened to Jesus would one day happen to them—that they, too, would share in His bodily resurrection and the power of God would transform their earthly bodies into the likeness of Christ!

The idea here simply cannot be that God wants us to be "spiritual" as opposed to grounded in the earth, or to go around with our heads in the clouds. Instead for Paul *flesh* is shorthand for a life that is disconnected from the source. *Flesh* is the way of a person whose desires have not yet been altered by grace, a person given to following his basest and lowest instincts instead of being called to a higher nature. *Flesh* is the way of self where the only thing that matters is *me* getting what *I* want, at anyone and everyone else's expense.

Simply put, when you are walking "in the flesh," your priorities are not God, the things of God, and the people of God. Your priority is pleasure; it's doing whatever makes you feel good at the moment. It is opposed to the way of God because it is not the way of humility, gentleness, and self-sacrifice—it's the way of dominating, winning, coercing, asserting your own will, and getting what you want, regardless of how it impacts anyone else. It's an entire way of life, intrinsically and inevitably in opposition to the way of grace.

But when a person is saved, she is no longer in the realm of the flesh—though very much still in her body, which is fearfully and wonderfully made, created in the image of God, intended for good, and intended to be fully restored! Within six months of becoming a Christian, I remember noticing I simply did not want to do many of the things I wanted to do before, and my old desires were being gradually replaced with new ones. It wasn't a matter of gritting my teeth to do the right thing, with my body kicking and screaming every moment—my very affections, the deepest inward inclinations of heart, mind, and body, were shifting. Within a year of becoming a Christian, my whole life had completely changed.

If you are now no longer walking according to the flesh but walking in the Spirit, you care what God thinks about your life more than what anybody else thinks. You don't want to grieve or offend the Holy Spirit, for no other reason than that God is the first love of your heart. You want all that God has for you, and you want to become all that God says you are and can yet become.

Of course this doesn't mean you get it right every time or you never struggle with a desire for something less than what God has for you. But your default settings are changed. Pleasing God and living for God is the new normal. If there is a tie in your life, God wins it. As a pastor this is what concerns me about people living in a world as busy and demanding as ours—it can appear at times as if God loses most ties. When there is a social function, sport, or recreational opportunity that is scheduled at the same time as church or another important gathering of God's people, it is important to be discerning so that our lifestyle choices don't leave us regularly preferring things that ultimately will not build our faith.

I'm not proposing some new legalism here—only that part of what we must learn to do is to live the kind of life where we put God first, prioritize the things of God, and learn to orient our lives around God's will for us. If we do that, for ourselves and for our children, it will save so much unnecessary pain and heartache down the road! There is no way to do this without living in such a way that God wins the tie. That's training for life in the Spirit!

Life in the Spirit doesn't mean we don't attend to the world around us or aren't present for the people God has placed in our lives. It is quite the opposite: when we are delivered from the tyranny of the flesh and its disordered desires, we attend to the world around us *better*; we are *more* present for the people we love and who love us—not less!

## THE FRUIT OF THE SPIRIT

Life in the flesh—life disconnected from the Source—always ends in death. But on the other hand, if we walk in the Spirit, we are connected to the One who is the Source of all life and the Source of all that is life-giving. It's the kind of life Jesus describes in John 15:7: we abide in Him, and His words abide in us. We are branches connected to the Vine, and life can organically, naturally flow in us and through us. When we are connected to the Source, our lesser desires no longer dominate us. Instead, we start to bear good fruit—what Paul describes in Galatians as the fruit of the Spirit:

love, joy, peace, patience, kindness, goodness, faithfulness, gentleness, and self-control.

The real wonder of all of this is that our effort is not the determinative factor in our spiritual growth. We are not capable of producing the fruit of the Spirit. If we've lived long enough, we have already tasted the fruit we bear when we aimlessly do what we please, and that fruit is not good! Instead we are learning to simply live in a constant state of connectivity to the Source. When Paul elsewhere admonishes us to "pray without ceasing," the idea is not that we manically go around babbling out loud to God all day, but that prayer becomes our way of living in the world with God—a whole new way of *being*!

*Chapter 16*

# CONGRATULATIONS ON YOUR ADOPTION

For you did not receive a spirit of slavery to fall back into fear, but you have received a spirit of adoption. When we cry, "Abba! Father!" it is that very Spirit bearing witness with our spirit that we are children of God, and if children, then heirs, heirs of God and joint heirs with Christ—if, in fact, we suffer with him so that we may also be glorified with him.

—ROMANS 8:15–17, NRSV

J UST A FEW weeks before the trip during which I was overwhelmed by my own struggle with God's grace, we had buried my father.

Nothing ever fully prepares you to lose a parent, but the truth was that he really had lived an incredibly rich, full life. A hard-working farmer, my dad exemplified everything that was extraordinary about the greatest generation. He enlisted in the army and became a pilot instructor. He loved both farming and flying.

When he settled back into his life on the farm, he knew he wanted a big family, and he got one. The two things he was most passionate about were family and watching things grow, and his life was full of both. When our family gathered around the dinner table, there was always laughter. In that sense it always seemed to me that my dad enjoyed life more than most. In every sense of the word he was a deeply good man—honorable, kind, and generous.

But like many men of his generation, my father didn't talk freely about his emotions. That just wasn't the world he lived in. He was tough. Over and over again, whether battling aggressive prostate cancer or a double knee replacement, or continuing to bring in the harvest for two full days with a ruptured appendix, without attempting to be strong, my father exhibited a strength and toughness that I still hope to match someday. As you can tell, I admire much about him.

A couple of months before my father died, I was taken aback by a question one of my sisters asked me: "Has Dad ever told you he loved you?" The question surprised me. I honestly had never thought about it before. I wasn't sure I had ever heard him say the words. For my dad loving your children meant giving everything you had to provide for them, and he did that with every fiber of his being. In that sense, he loved us well. He would have done anything to keep us safe and ensure we had a future. Still, her question lingered in me, so I planned to bring it up with my dad the next time I saw him. For a father who wanted to provide for his kids, there was one thing he had left undone: giving the gift of verbally expressing his love. But before I could make it to Colorado to visit, he was gone.

Losing my dad seemed to break open all these questions. Because my dad was such a hero to me, I struggled to come to terms with the notion that my emotional connection with him didn't feel as deep as my heart wanted. For the first time in my life I could see I had my own version of a problem I've heard countless people in our church give voice to over the years: disentangling any shortcomings in my relationship with my earthly father from my relationship with the heavenly Father.

## OUR ADOPTION

Our salvation is so amazing and incredible that human words fail to describe the enormity of it, the wonder of it—the generosity of it. Like a diamond, the beauty of salvation is complex and multifaceted. So through the story of Scripture we are given many beautiful images and metaphors for what God has accomplished for us in our salvation—think of Noah and his family being kept safe from judgment through the ark God told him to build. Think of Jesus comparing our salvation to a vast celebration, the most epic wedding feast ever thrown; or also per the teaching of Jesus, think of the Good Shepherd who leaves the ninety-nine to go after the one lost sheep. All of these images dazzle and captivate us in their own way.

But for all the beauty and power resident in these images, the most significant, most gripping, most powerful picture of what God has done for us (I would even say *the best!*) is given to us in Romans 8—our salvation as *adoption*. Verses 14–17 say, "For all who are led by the Spirit of God are sons of God. For you did not receive the spirit of slavery to fall back into fear, but you have received the Spirit of adoption as sons, by whom we cry, 'Abba! Father!' The Spirit himself bears witness with our spirit that we are children of God, and if children, then heirs—heirs of God and fellow heirs with Christ." Try to comprehend for a moment something of this magnitude. God adopted you. And according to Paul in Ephesians 1:4, He decided to do this "before the foundation of the world." It was a plan so ancient and intentional that it actually predates time as we know it.

Adoption is a legal action by which a person or persons take into their family a child not their own and give them all the privileges of their own child. It is a beautiful concept in any culture at any time, but the particular nuances of adoption in Paul's time make this rich image all the more powerful. In Paul's time an adopted child actually had more privilege than a biological child. There was a different kind of intentionality to it. You weren't just born into a family; you were chosen to be part of that family!

One of the foundations of the Roman family unit was the notion of *patria potestas*, "the father's power." It meant that the father had absolute power over his children—he could even choose to kill them without recourse or penalty if he wanted. If your father said you lived, you lived. If your father said you died, you died. And the father's absolute power lasted his entire lifetime. A child would never grow beyond that. You can see how that principle would make adoption all the more difficult—unless of course a child was an orphan or born into slavery, in which case he had no legal rights, and anything could be done with him.

But if a man saw a son that belonged to another father and wanted him—perhaps he felt his own biological sons were not worthy or up for the task of managing his estate—he could adopt another male as his son. In our cultural context it is a hard practice to fathom, but it was perfectly common in the Roman Empire. In fact, the Roman emperors of Paul's time comprised basically a who's who list of adopted sons: Julius Caesar adopted Augustus Caesar. Augustus Caesar adopted Tiberius. Trajan was adopted, Hadrian was adopted, and Marcus Aurelius was adopted, to name a few. There were many more.

The Roman adoption process followed two steps. The first step was *mancipatio,* from which we get our word *emancipation.* That phase of adoption involved a symbolic sale that dramatized the entire act, to be carried out in the presence of witnesses. You would bring a scale and have some gold coins or copper coins. The father of the child to be adopted would act out selling his son on the scale, then act out buying back his son, then act out selling his son again, and then act out buying back his son again. But on the third time the father sold his son without buying the son back, and his rights were symbolically severed. The second stage of adoption was called *vindicatio. Vindicatio* is the phase when the adopting father went to a Roman magistrate and presented the case for legal adoption, which had to be witnessed by seven people. (Note that parallel to this the Book of Revelation refers to the Holy Spirit as the sevenfold spirit/spirits of God. See Revelation 1:4; 3:1; 4:5; 5:6.)

There were quite tangible consequences of the adoption. First of all, the adopted person lost all rights to his own family and gained all rights in his new family. Second, the adopted person became the full heir to his new father's estate, even if there were other sons. In other words, he didn't just share in the inheritance; he got all of the inheritance. Third, the adopted person's old life was completely wiped out. If there were debts, they were canceled. If there was a record of crime, it was expunged. It was as if the previous person had never existed (incidentally, the adoption didn't necessarily happen with children, although it could. Oftentimes adults were adopted!). Thus, in the eyes of Roman law in society, it was as if the adopted person was literally and completely the son of his new father in every sense.[1]

Take a moment now and attempt to fathom the implications of this in terms of how God adopts you! You lost all rights to your old family (the family of Adam, laboring under the curse, convicted and constrained by the law). You gained all the rights of your new family—the actual *family of God*! In Christ you now have all the rights as if you were God's child by birth. You are now a full heir to your new Father's estate, even if He has other sons. It is all yours, all given to you as an heir of God and coheir with Christ.

We are not part-heirs but fully adopted as sons and daughters of God! Our old lives and any vestiges of our old identity are wiped out entirely. The record is expunged, and all debts are paid. It's as if that person never existed. In Roman culture, law and society recognized the adopted person as a full-fledged son of his new father in every sense.

## THE ROLE OF THE SPIRIT IN OUR ADOPTION

This is what happens when God saves us. We are accepted as God's children in every way, without exception. The Spirit of God Himself bears witness to and is actively involved in our adoption. That Spirit, the Holy Spirit, bears witness with our spirit that we are the children of God. Specifically, as Paul put it in Romans 8:14, "For all who are led by the Spirit of God are sons of God."

In our own cultural context the gendered language here can sound problematic. But keep in mind it is this same apostle Paul who uttered perhaps the most radical words spoken in his time and place in history, that in Christ we are "neither male nor female" (Gal. 3:28, NKJV). There is no distinction between sons and daughters in God; both are full heirs! Sonship remains the touchstone here because at the time Paul was writing, only male children had claims on inheritance. The implication is that whether male or female, in Christ we are the full beneficiaries of God's inheritance!

Now the same Spirit who led Jesus into the wilderness leads us wherever we go. We are not orphans left to our own devices, trying to figure out where we should go and what we are supposed to do. The Spirit comes as our guide to teach us, instruct us, convict us, and direct us. The Spirit whispers the mysteries of God to us, guiding us, in the words of Jesus, "into all truth" (John 16:13, NKJV).

And finally, the Spirit of God, according to Paul in Romans 8:15, does away with "the spirit of slavery," replacing all our old anxieties with "the Spirit of adoption as sons, by whom we cry, 'Abba! Father!'" The Greek word *Abba* was the most intimate term of endearment, a childlike term similar to *Daddy* or *Papa*. We now have a childlike intimacy with God, given to us by the Holy Spirit. The Spirit of God stays with us now, reminding us of who we are and of what God has already said about us.

It's as if you received a letter in the mail informing you of a rich uncle you had never met. The letter says he passed away and his will has been found. As it turns out, that uncle happened to be number one on *Forbes'* list of richest people in the world, and he decided to bequeath his entire fortune to you!

The Spirit delivers this very news to us. We even have it in writing—that is exactly what Scripture is, the letter that comes special delivery to reveal to us the best news we've ever heard: that we are now named as full heirs of God! The Holy Spirit both delivers and confirms this amazing news.

God made the decision to give you this inheritance long before you were ever born. It was God's plan all along—it has nothing to do with us and is not contingent on us. All we are asked to do is receive and cooperate with the work God has already done. God has done all the heavy lifting. All that we need to do is say yes and surrender to Him.

When people think about the inheritance we have in Christ, they are often inclined to think of heaven—to think of mansions in the sky or streets of gold. But what we are given in the kingdom of God is far greater than any tangible gift we could receive. For we aren't just given all of our Father's good gifts—we are given the Giver Himself. God is our portion, our inheritance, our reward! The One who hovers over us and sings over us with delight is now ours, and we are His. And the beautiful thing is that we don't have to wait until we die to enjoy Him. He is here with us even now, His love sustaining us with every breath. We can delight in Him now, as He always delights in us. He celebrates us for who we are and how we are created. And it doesn't have anything to do with what we have or haven't done—God delights in us simply because we exist!

Now every time we experience the joy and wonder of the Holy Spirit in worship, or when we sense God's presence in the beauty of nature or the love of another human being— every time we get a whiff of that presence, in large or small ways, it is a divine foretaste of heaven. It is a glimpse—and only a glimpse, because we cannot yet handle more—of the glory that is to come. In fact, the sheer joy that awaits us is so full and intense that we will need renewed, glorified bodies just to have the capacity to receive it all! The Holy Spirit reminds us of not only what God has already done for us in Christ but also what God will yet do in completing the good work He has begun in us.

## AN EPILOGUE

I told you that my own father was a deeply good man who, as a man of his generation, couldn't easily put his heart into words. I'm happy to be able to say that whatever emotional distance I might have sensed there, any crevice in me that wasn't quite filled because I rarely actually heard affectionate words from him, has been more than filled by my Father in heaven. Specifically, as I've walked this road of grace through Romans, the Father's love has been illumined to me on every page, in every line of every verse. God has been so good to speak His words of affirmation and acceptance over me.

But I have to tell you that while my father was not an especially verbal or emotional person, I had the joy of seeing a profound change in his life. As much as he loved us in his own way, always providing for us, and certainly respected the call of God on my life, he never became a Christian himself. My mom prayed for his salvation for twenty-five years. He would ask me spiritual questions sometimes, but he just never seemed ready to make the leap to trust God for himself.

And then, at the age of seventy-eight, he came to James River on Easter Sunday. In a moment I'll never forget, my father raised his hand to receive Christ. In all of my years I only saw my dad cry one time—the moment he heard his mother had passed away. But at church that day he cried freely. He was my father, but I got to witness his adoption into the family of God.

A year later my dad's lifelong friend was dying of throat cancer. The cancer was so advanced that the man could no longer speak. When my dad came to see him, he told him about his own experience, about how God had saved him. He asked his friend if he would like to receive Christ. Since he could not speak, his friend squeezed his hand to say *yes*, and they prayed together.

It just goes to show, no matter how old you are, how much life is behind you, who you are or what you've done—you're never too old to be adopted.

## Chapter 17

# GOD IS WORKING IN ALL THINGS

And we know that for those who love God all things work together for good, for those who are called according to his purpose.

—ROMANS 8:28

PAUL HAS GIVEN us a staggering view of grace—grace that has broken into the world already through Jesus Christ and is still breaking in. That kingdom was inaugurated when He came the first time, and it is established in the world already. But while the rule and reign of God's kingdom is available in the present, in another sense it is still "not yet." For two thousand years Christians have been praying the prayer the Lord gave us in Matthew 6:10 (NIV): "your kingdom come, your will be done, on earth as it is in heaven." We trust and believe that day is coming, but it has not yet come in fullness. We live in the tension between the already and not yet, beneficiaries of what Christ has done but patiently waiting on that which He will yet do.

We live in the ambiguity of the in-between. There is hope, but there is also pain on this part of the journey. There is a deep groaning and sighing for what is yet to come—Paul says creation itself is groaning for redemption. As believers we, along with creation, are experiencing the pains of labor.

I'll never forget the first time I ever preached on a Sunday morning. It was September 30 of 1984. It's impossible to forget because of what had happened the day before. Debbie and I were living in a duplex. After we got up that morning, she told me, "I think we'd better get in the car and go to the hospital. I'm having contractions." We feverishly gathered our things, jumped in the car, and rushed to the hospital.

When we got there, labor and delivery was completely jammed. I can still remember the sound of a woman screaming while we were checking in. I looked at Debbie—her eyes were getting wide. When the nurse finally examined her, she told her that she didn't think she was ready and that we should go back home.

We pleaded with the nurse to let us stay at the hospital. They only had one room left, and the nurse reluctantly agreed to let Debbie stay until they needed the space for someone closer to delivery. We finally got her checked in. I ran to the nearby bank to get some quarters so I could make phone calls to share the good news. (For younger readers, this was in the days before cell phones, when we had something called a pay phone. If you don't know what that is, I'm sure you can see one at the Smithsonian now.)

By the time I got back to the room, we were able to sit and talk calmly. Debbie's contractions had almost completely stopped. I was fully present for her, but in the back of my mind I couldn't help but start to get anxious about preaching Sunday morning. So we got down on our knees in that little room and I prayed, "God, I am supposed to preach tomorrow morning. My sermon isn't written yet, so if You wouldn't mind, we need to have this baby by noon. In Jesus' name, amen." Sure enough, in less than an hour the contractions came with intensity.

We were a young couple and had gone through the birthing classes together, but it was our first rodeo—and of course, nothing really prepares you for that! The birthing classes had laid out my responsibility—I was the coach, and my job was to help Debbie control her breathing. As her labor intensified, I hovered over her face, telling her in her my most soothing Zen voice, "Debbie, you have to breathe. This will help you!"

Instantly she looked back up at me and said, "*Would you please be quiet!*" My labor coaching days ended quickly and without a lot of fanfare. (Though, gratefully, Jonathan David Lindell was born healthy on September 29!)

There was only so much comfort I could have provided to Debbie at that moment because she was in the midst of labor pains—intense, volatile, painful. It is that same imagery the apostle Paul has in mind in Romans 8. God is now in the process of completing this work of making us new and bringing His kingdom to bear in the world—it is at times painful and can involve suffering. But like the pain of childbirth, it is temporary.

God has already begun His good work in us and has promised to be faithful to complete it. And we know that when we are glorified and fully conformed to the image of Jesus, we have nothing but glory ahead. But in this messy middle, this in-between time, suffering is a reality. Paul says, "For I consider that the sufferings of this present time are not worth comparing with the glory that is to be revealed to us" (Rom. 8:18). The pain is minuscule compared to the beauty that awaits us.

In the meantime, as we navigate the complexities of the "already but not yet," God gives His sons and daughters specific promises that can sustain us. We are not promised a carefree, easy road. But grace is not just ahead of us—it is at work here, now, assuring us that we aren't alone and that God is going to finish what He started.

## ALL THINGS WORK TOGETHER

It is one of the most beloved, treasured verses in all of Scripture: "And we know that for those who love God all things work together for good, for those who are called according to his purpose" (Rom. 8:28). It should be noted that this promise is specifically for believers—it is a hope reserved for those who are in Christ. It is not that God does not care about those who are not yet in Christ or that He does not long to heal and bless them. It is His desire, according to Jesus, that "none would perish." But this promise simply does not make sense outside the context of salvation.

The truth is, some kinds of suffering don't seem to have a sense of meaning or purpose unless that suffering is understood in the context of the long game, what God is doing in eternity. Not all suffering is redemptive insofar that it immediately yields some kind of value or lesson that makes it seem worthwhile. If this life was all we had, and there was no hope beyond the grave, many trials would seem to be without particular meaning. But if those trials are placed against the larger backdrop of where God is taking us on the journey of salvation—from new birth to consummation, when we are glorified and God's rule is made complete in us—suffering takes on a sense of purpose it could not have had before. Whatever happens to us from the time we first encounter Christ forward is part of a larger story of how God is making us new.

If we are in Christ, the really astonishing thing is just how vast and comprehensive the scope of this promise really is. *"All things* work together for good…" All things, anything, and everything, without exception—every single thing that we experience, both that which brings joy and laughter and that which would seem to threaten to destroy or undo us— all of it is working together for good. Nothing is wasted, not a single tear or sorrow. The good things, the bad things, the disappointing things, the frustrating things, the tragic things, the difficult things, the stressful things, the happy things—nothing is left out of God's master plan of shaping us into the image of the Son.

The Greek word *sunergeo* is where we get the word *synergy*. For the Christian there is an essential synergy to all of life. Even the notes that seem dissonant are coming together to be part of a beautiful symphony. God is working for us and in us, not through *some* things but *all* things!

There is nothing so dark or difficult that God cannot harness it, leverage it, and repurpose it for your good. That does not mean God directly scripts every hardship in your life; rather, it is the very nature and character of God to always be at work bringing beauty out of brokenness in your life. Nothing is beyond His purview. The most dark and difficult things that you have experienced in your life—from abuse to car accidents to cancer—are transformed and transfigured in such a way that God uses them to bring healing and wholeness to others who are facing them now. As Henri Nouwen taught, God actually heals through our wounds, just as God brought us healing through the wounds of Jesus on the cross.[1]

Even the temptation or sin that you struggle with most violently can be leveraged to make you more dependent on God and His grace. Instead of pushing you further away, your weaknesses have a way of drawing you closer to Jesus, serving only to make you more aware of your need for Him. In the words of Joseph in the Old Testament, what your enemy has intended for evil, God has used for good. (See Genesis 50:20.) Don't be deceived into thinking there is anything in your life that God cannot and will not use to bring about His good purposes!

## WORKS IN PROGRESS

While I believe God is not the architect of all of our pain, and that it breaks God's heart to see His children suffer, I also believe there is nothing God cannot or will not use to bring His good purposes to bear in us. Even the very worst things.

In 1998 we were getting ready to build our South Campus at James River Church. My best friend was a key leader in the church at the time, skilled in construction and a savvy businessman. He had agreed to be the liaison between us and the construction company to build this 196,000-square-foot building with a 3,500-seat sanctuary.

Like most everything we have done at James River, this building was going to be a faith journey. We were a church of young, middle-income families who gave generously but had limited finances. Six months into the project the construction company notified us that their bid on our project was off by millions of dollars and they would need to meet as soon as possible to resolve the situation.

Thankfully it was Wednesday when we received the news, which meant our church would be gathering that evening for the most important service of the week, the prayer meeting. The church prayed, and I knew the Lord was going to help us. Following the service I spoke with my friend at length about solutions to our construction dilemma. I went home thanking God for His presence in the church and for surrounding me with people who could help.

The next morning my friend's daughter called on the phone: "My dad is gone!" In a matter of minutes I was at his office, which was now surrounded by yellow crime tape. There was blood on the wall. His office had been ransacked. His car was gone. We searched the whole area, working with law enforcement, desperate to find out what happened to him. We found out later that he had actually faked his own disappearance. He had started a relationship with someone else and had schemed to start a new life hundreds of miles away.

We were all devastated. On a personal level I grieved the loss of my best friend. In the meantime, all kinds of rumors were circulating through the city about why he left and what had happened. I was trying to manage the grief and confusion in our congregation while trying to somehow manage the grief and confusion in me. There would be much of that work left ahead, but in the immediate aftermath I had a disastrous construction project on my hands that simply had to move forward.

I am not the builder nor the son of a builder. Our staff was still fairly small. But there was no way to turn back. We needed the Lord to come through in a big way to help us finish the building in a way we could afford while being in the midst of a public spectacle. Looking back on that season, I am still amazed at God's miraculous provision. By the time we moved into the building, we had already paid two-thirds of the total cost! I still have a large picture hanging in our office suite from 1999 that shows the building sitting in a field of mud created by spring rains that wouldn't quit. The architect had commissioned a flyover picture and titled it, "A work in progress." I've kept it all these years as a reminder that no matter how bleak the situation or how overwhelming the circumstances, our church and my life are still works in progress.

That picture also reminds me of the faithfulness of God. It wasn't long until the church doubled in attendance, and then doubled again. As difficult as that whole season was corporately and personally, it made us all the more dependent on God's grace—and grace came through in a big way. It is not despite all our detours, tragedies, and missteps that God works out His purposes for our lives—but straight through them; all things working together for good, to those who love Him!

## THE PROCESS OF SALVATION BROUGHT TO COMPLETION

The only way we can call it all "good" in a way that makes sense is in the context of the broader story of salvation. Paul puts this glorious promise within the framework of the story of redemption, which—no matter what kind of story you feel your life is telling right now—is the story God is telling of your life:

> And we know that for those who love God all things work together for good, for those who are called according to his purpose. For those whom he foreknew he also predestined to be conformed to the image of his Son, in order that he might be the firstborn among many brothers. And those whom he predestined he also called, and those whom he called he also justified, and those whom he justified he also glorified.
>
> —ROMANS 8:28–30

It is an outline of the process of salvation. As we saw before, in Christ you are saved, are being saved, and will be saved!

As it is with anything in Scripture and in life, it all begins and ends with God. It began with God's foreknowledge. This foreknowledge is not merely foresight. The meteorologist on the evening news has a limited ability to predict what the weather will or will not do based on patterns that go before.

But God has a much more intimate kind of knowledge, a knowing of the heart as much as the mind. The Hebrew word *yada* (to know) always implies an intimate knowledge, an experiential knowledge—a relational knowledge. Adam "knew" Eve; Cain "knew" his wife.

In Amos 3:2 God said to Israel, "You only have I known." Clearly God's chosen people weren't the only ones He knew *about*. But these were His cherished sons and daughters, His beloved, His chosen ones. They were the ones with whom He had relationship, the ones He was passionate about and cared about. Practically speaking, foreknowledge is synonymous with love. We could read Romans 8:29 this way: "For those whom he *fore-loved*..."

Deuteronomy 7:7 articulates this especially beautifully: "It was not because you were more in number than any other people that the LORD set his love on you and chose you, for you were the fewest of all peoples." In other words, you weren't the strongest, wisest, most attractive, or best—this was never contingent on you, never about your worthiness or unworthiness, your goodness or your lack thereof. This was always about God's goodness, God's beauty, and God's decision before time to love you!

Again, Romans 8:29 says, "For those whom he foreknew he also predestined to be conformed to the image of his Son." The word *predestined* means to decide beforehand or to predetermine. This theme permeates all of Paul's teaching, constantly pausing to wonder at the way God chose us. He wrote in Ephesians 1:4–5, "In love he predestined us for adoption...through Jesus Christ, according to the purpose of his will."

It is important to note here that biblically speaking,

foreknowledge and predestination should only be understood positively. You cannot take the positive truth that God loved and chose those who are in Christ to say conversely that those who are not yet in Christ were not loved and chosen. Scripture does not draw this conclusion. People who reject God and God's salvation do so out of their own free will, which He will not override to drag them kicking and screaming into a bliss they do not choose. Their rejection is not based on God's predetermined decision.

People will ask, "But how can one be true and not the other?" Admittedly this mystery, this tension is beyond us to resolve. The relationship between God's sovereign act of choosing us and human free will is complex and multifaceted, which is why Christians have been having family disputes about these matters for two thousand years. There are plenty of things about the sovereign ways of God that we cannot understand intellectually.

Yet what does the Book of Romans work in us, as well as our own experience of knowing and walking with God over time? That God is good, and God is trustworthy. We can count on Him, and we can depend on Him. When we cannot discern His ways or figure out His methods, we can trust His heart—we can trust His good intentions for us!

And what did God predetermine or predestine? That we would be called. That this decision to love us and know us— the thoughts God had of you before there was a you to think about—would intersect with space and time in such a way that God would step into human history and call you out, draw you out, and summon you to Himself.

Like those first fisherman disciples who dropped their nets to follow Jesus, there was a moment in time when you heard God whisper your name. It was not a generic summons to humanity, but a personal, individual, tailored invitation; a moment when you realized not only that He knows and calls you by name, but that He knows everything about you, everything there is to know—all the things about you that you do not know and cannot know.

Those that God called, then, He justified. This is what much of the early chapters were about: how God makes you right and made you righteous by clothing you in the righteousness of God; covering all of your shame with His redeeming love; giving you His own robe and ring and sandals, like the father of the prodigal son.

You were forgiven, cleansed, and given a new identity. Old things passed away, and you became something new. You were still you in the sense that you had the same nose, eyes, mouth, and a semblance of your old personality; but you were also a whole new you, with a new nature, a new identity and purpose, and a slate wiped clean.

And then finally, we will be glorified. In a split second mortality will be swallowed up into immortality. God doesn't start anything He will not complete. Paul writes in Philippians 1:6 (NIV), "He who began a good work in you will carry it on to completion until the day of Christ Jesus." What had begun simply as an intention in the heart of God comes to fruition and fullness. In the words of 1 John 3:2 (NIV), "What we will be has not yet been made known. But we know that when Christ appears, we shall be like him, for we shall see him as he is."

As I said, the joy that God has for us on the other side of the veil is so intense, we will need new bodies in order to contain it!

*Chapter 18*

# MORE THAN CONQUERORS

No, in all these things we are more than conquerors through him who loved us.

—ROMANS 8:37, NIV

**M**ANY CHRISTIANS CAN imagine nothing better for themselves than a life of mere survival. The road can be long and arduous. We all certainly know what it is to feel undone and defeated, to be at the end of ourselves. Paul was not naïve or unrealistic about how challenging life can be—even life with God. He was a man all too acquainted with pain, heartbreak, betrayal, and even physical torture. He never promised us that a life in Christ would make us somehow exempt from hardship and tragedy. He never told us that following Jesus would keep us from cancer, car accidents, or failed relationships. He could write intelligibly about "nakedness, famine, and sword" and facing resistance from principalities and powers because he wrote from hard-edged, first-person experience! (See Romans 8:35.)

And yet it is not *despite* all these things that befall us, but precisely "*in* all these things" that Paul utters these defiant, triumphant words: "We are more than conquerors through him who loved us" (Rom. 8:37). He did not say we are survivors, though some of us have survived unbelievably intense trials in which surviving was no small thing. Knowing all the pain that Paul tasted, for him to be able to say, "We are conquerors," would be remarkable enough. But he didn't even say we are conquerors; he said that in Christ we are "*more* than conquerors"!

So many of us settle for barely enough or just enough. But we have a quality of life in Jesus that goes past victory, a kind of overcoming that transcends our darkest moments and most difficult trials. It is not contingent on our circumstances, our context, whether or not things break our way, or whether or not the people we care about stand by us. Like everything else in the life of grace, it is a pure gift that doesn't require our effort, only our cooperation—to allow our defeats to be swallowed up in Jesus' death on the cross, and to be carried into His victory through the resurrection.

## CLOSING ARGUMENTS

As the greatest manifesto on grace ever written began to climax in Romans 8:1, we read these stunning words: "There is therefore now no condemnation for those who are in Christ Jesus." Most Christians have heard this scripture before, but the words bring only a passing joy at best. It comes down to a fundamental lack of understanding of grace. And because so many Christians don't understand grace, in turn they don't understand God's commitment to their salvation, which started before time began and will extend into eternity when time is no more. They don't realize the lengths to which God has gone to bring His sons and daughters home. They don't comprehend that salvation is more than just forgiveness. They don't fathom the devastating power of sin, nor the dominating force of grace! They don't understand how the Holy Spirit makes them like Jesus.

Consequently they feel condemned—either by God or by themselves. The tragedy is that they waste their time feeling alienated from God, trying to keep rules to please God, or continually starting over in their walk with God. Not to mention the fact that they forfeit the incredible joy and strength that come from not only hearing but actually experiencing the good news of the gospel!

As we come to Romans 8:31–39, the conclusion of the letter, we hear the good news in full force, without restraint. Like a brilliant attorney Paul begins the closing argument on his case for grace. He anticipates every objection that could be brought to his case, every argument that might be levied. In a flourish of soaring rhetoric, he brings it home.

Paul knew all too well what it was to have people against him. He'd had the government against him, Caesar against him, his fellow Jews against him, and even fellow Christians against him! He knew what it was to be accused, mocked, and talked about. The experience he had with Jesus on the Damascus road did not spare him from any and all kinds of opposition. Following Jesus intensified the opposition! But in response Paul thunders back, "If God is for us, who can be against us?" (v. 31).

No matter who else may turn on us, criticize us, misunderstand us, judge us, or label us, the verdict has already been rendered once and for all: God is permanently, completely, irrevocably *for us*. The One who spoke all of creation into existence by a whisper is on our side. He is not temperamental, flaky, moody, or insecure; He is not for us on some days and against us on others. He doesn't get worn out or exasperated with us. No matter who else resists us, the posture of God is for us and only for us, in all times, places, and circumstances. And if God is for and with us, who can be against us? No matter how much power or influence the opposition might have—even if it is Caesar—who could overcome the God of the universe, who has already decided to be forever on our side?

If we have any question as to how far God will go to fulfill His good purposes for us, we need only look at what He has already been willing to do: "He who did not spare his own Son but gave him up for us all, how will he not also with him graciously give us all things?" (v. 32). In other words, if God was willing to sacrifice His own Son in order to redeem and rescue us, is there anything He wouldn't do for us? If He has already gone so far as to sacrifice all that He loved to bring us home, what would He possibly withhold from us? The cross has already demonstrated God's willingness to go to any length for us; there is no expense spared.

This all sounds wonderful, of course. But even with all that God has done for us, we all know what it is to feel accused, blamed, and even at times ashamed. It would be one thing if we were innocent, pure, and sinless—if we always got it right. Over the course of our lives we will at times face accusation from others, but often the greater difficulty is in dealing with the accusation from ourselves.

If our consciences aren't accusing us, then Satan himself takes up the role, since he is the accuser of the brethren. It is his job description—it's an office, a role. But it is not just what he does; it's who he is. He is the accuser, "*the* Satan." Accusation is who he is and what he is; it is what sustains him. And it can seem as if he has infinite leverage to use against us: all the mistakes we've made, all the times we have failed, fallen, and disappointed someone else or ourselves. In response to all of this Paul fires back: "Who shall bring any charge against God's elect? It is God who justifies" (v. 33).

Paul writes in the language of a legal challenge. The heavenly court is open to hear any charges that could be brought against us. Our relationship with God is not only a personal one but also a legal one—God is our Judge. But all of our punishment was placed on Jesus on the cross. He bore our penalty for us; our debt has been paid.

The One who judges us is the One who loves us with an everlasting love, and He has already justified us. He has already declared us forgiven, righteous, and holy. It's all the more extraordinary because we were, in fact, guilty! But the God who is rich in mercy satisfied the demands by taking our place, bearing our sin, suffering the punishment that we deserved, and rendering the forever verdict that we are clean and free. Who cares what anybody else says when God has paid the debt and satisfied the charges that have been brought against us? We are righteous in the sight of God because God has already said so—and that truth is established for eternity. No one can challenge it, much less change it!

Sure, we still hear the voice of the accuser in the distance sometimes, yapping at our heels like a tiny Chihuahua (and no more of a threat). But the time will come, Revelation 12:10 (NIV) tells us, when "the accuser of our brothers and sisters, who accuses them before our God day and night, [is] hurled down." Already his voice has no power over us and his accusations have no weight. The more we remind ourselves of the truth of who God says we are, the fainter the enemy's voice becomes. But the day will come when he will be utterly silenced and we will never have another accusation ring in our ears, never have an endless instant replay of past mistakes on loop in our minds.

Do not forget that God's decision to justify you was not an afterthought or a plan B. God foreknew you, chose you, and predestined you. Maybe you know how it feels to not be chosen on the playground in grade school. Perhaps you know what it is like to not make the team, not get the job, or to be passed over for the promotion. Maybe you know what it is to feel left out, unseen, or overlooked. Maybe that is how you have walked through life, and consequently, how you have come to live the spiritual life. But God called you out from the rest, loved you first, and loved you best. You were never a second or third choice to the Love that calls you by name. You are who God wants! You are God's *chosen* from eternity past.

## WHO WILL CONDEMN US?

But God's grace doesn't stop there. "Who is to condemn?" Satan's accusations are powerless against us. For most of us, however, the real threat of condemnation is not external but internal. Sometimes it is not Satan's condemnation that we can't seem to get out from under but our own. Scripture anticipates this, which is why the apostle John, who, like Paul, was a man utterly swept up by amazing grace, wrote these words: "Dear friends, if our hearts do not condemn us, we have confidence before God and receive from him anything we ask, because we keep his commands and do what pleases him" (1 John 3:21–22, NIV). Our hearts know things about us that others do not know. John doesn't encourage us to ignore those thoughts that are generated in our hearts but to meet them by realizing God knows more!

God is not less acquainted with our failures and short-comings than we are, but much more so. He knows them better than we do and can see us so much more clearly than we can see ourselves. God has access to all the information, to every mangled motive and even the slightest self-deception. He knows all of this and more. And yet God also knows the sacrifice His Son already made for us and the verdict already rendered. He knows how completely He loves us. So if our hearts do condemn us, what should we do? In that moment we rest in the fact that God's judgments are infinitely higher than our judgments, and God is greater than our hearts!

Paul continues, "Christ Jesus is the one who died—more

than that, who was raised—who is at the right hand of God, who indeed is interceding for us" (Rom. 8:34). In contrast to Satan, who is the accuser, Jesus is our Advocate, our Defender—the One who pleads our case.

Some preachers have had a good time with this idea, painting colorful scenes of a heavenly courtroom, with Satan as the prosecutor pointing out our sin, demanding the Father condemn, only to have Jesus interrupt to remind the Father, "I died for them! Their sins are forgiven." As if somehow the Father could forget what Jesus did! Nothing could be further from Paul's imagery here. His emphasis in Romans 8 is on how the entire Trinity—Father, Son, and Spirit—are constantly working together for our good and the furtherance of their purpose for us.

God the Father does not have dementia. He does not get confused about what to do with you when you stumble. He chose you before the foundations of the world. He has already declared you to be righteous and forgiven. Whatever interceding is, it has nothing to do with Jesus needing to remind the Father that our sin has been washed away. The Book of Hebrews tells us that because Jesus was tempted as a man, He is sympathetic to our weaknesses. He understands the frailty of the human condition in an experiential, first-person way. In the words of Psalm 103:14, "He remembers that we are dust."

He is not detached or distant from us. He knows that life on earth is no cakewalk. He knows what it means to be tired, hungry, misunderstood, and rejected. He is able to enter into solidarity with us, to be moved by that which moves us, touched by that which touches us.

In Jesus we have an Advocate who is willing to stand between us and any and all who would accuse us. In John 8 the Pharisees dragged a half-naked woman out of a bed she shared with a man who was not her husband. In a clearly premeditated scheme they had laid a trap for her—and for Jesus, trying to corner Him into publicly contradicting the law. As they dragged her into the presence of Love Himself, she trembled, weeping, her face red with shame. The Pharisees reminded Jesus that the law demands such a person be stoned, and they asked Him what they should do with her.

Jesus did not open His mouth at first. He bent down, wrote in the dirt, and then looked up and said, "Let him who is without sin among you be the first to throw a stone at her" (v. 7). His response stunned the mob, who at first could only stand and stare.

Slowly, one by one, beginning with the older men who had lived too much to feign sinlessness, her accusers walked away. With tenderness in His eyes Jesus asked her softly, "Where are they? Has no one condemned you?"

"No one, Lord," she responded through shaking lips.

"Neither do I condemn you; go, and from now on sin no more." (See John 8:1–11.)

In this powerful scene, Christ reveals a definitive portrait of God to us. Jesus stands between the accused and her accusers, absorbing their rage. He stands there protecting a cherished, wayward daughter of God, as He stands for us now. In Jesus we see a God who is willing to stand between our accuser and us. Simply put—Jesus is the God who always has your back!

## THE VERDICT IS IN

Now, all the evidence has been entered. When you look at it in total, it is staggering. The proof of God's love is overwhelming: God is for you! No one can bring a charge against you, much less condemn you now. (Not even you!) Given the extreme lengths to which God has gone to bring you home, how could you possibly deny His love for you now?

So now hear the holy hush in the court as Paul brings his argument to its logical conclusion. "For I am sure that neither death nor life, nor angels nor rulers, nor things present nor things to come, nor powers, nor height nor depth, nor anything else in all creation, will be able to separate us from the love of God in Christ Jesus our Lord" (Rom. 8:38–39).

In the language of the King James Version, Paul starts with "For I am *persuaded*." The question is, are you persuaded? The evidence leaves no room for any doubt as to how God feels about you. With all that God has done to demonstrate His love for you, what could separate you now? Paul's list is comprehensive in scope:

*Neither death*—if you kill me, I will be even closer to Christ. Paul said he preferred "to be absent from the body and to be present with the Lord" (2 Cor. 5:8, NKJV).

*Nor life*—if I live, I'll live for Him and experience no distance from Him.

*Nor angels*—they will only help me follow Christ.

*Nor rulers (demons)*—they must flee at the name of Jesus.

*Nor things present*—no matter the obstacle in front of me, "I can do all things through Christ who strengthens me" (Phil. 4:13, NKJV).

*Nor things to come*—"'for I know the plans I have for you,' declares the LORD, 'plans to prosper you and not to harm you, plans to give you hope and a future'" (Jer. 29:11, NIV).

*Nor powers*—Jesus is the power behind all powers. "All

things were created through Him and for Him" (Col. 1:16, NKJV).

*Nor height*—for what could be higher than Him? In the words of Ephesians 1:21 (NKJV), He is "far above all principality and power and might and dominion."

*Nor depth*—for on that first Easter, He descended into hell, proclaimed liberty to the captives, ascended on high, and "led captivity captive" (Eph. 4:8, NKJV).

*Nor anything else in all creation*—in spite of his trademark eloquence, Paul has simply run out of words. There is nothing more to say, except this:

> [*Nothing*] will be able to separate us from the love of God in Christ Jesus our Lord.
>
> —ROMANS 8:39

And with that, the case is closed: you are permanently, desperately, and entirely loved; the triune work of grace is able to overcome each and every scheme and attack that comes against you. Nothing and no one can separate you from His perfect love, and nothing and no one ever will. Come what may, God is going to complete the work He started in you. Before time began the Father set His heart on you and chose you; Jesus gave up everything to come and rescue you; and the Spirit lives in you, making you like Jesus—all of it a work of grace, and all of it summed up in the word *grace*.

## AN INVITATION

Romans is a brilliant book. But for all of its genius, it would be tragic to see it as just "heady" at its core; it is first and foremost heart. Specifically, it lays bare the heart of God—a God who knows everything there is to know about you, the good, the bad, and the ugly, but loves you anyway. For all the beautiful ideas it reveals about justification, sanctification, and glorification, I hope that most of all, you walk away with a revelation of the Father's heart.

He is for you. There has never been a moment of your life when He wasn't thinking about you. There is nothing He would not give to get to you. He chose you and loved you before you took your first breath. And as you navigate this life, He will never stop reaching out to you in love.

Romans makes it clear that by putting your faith in Jesus, you can experience more than just forgiveness of sin. Forgiveness of sin is wonderful, but your salvation is so much more! You are now a completely new person, one who is righteous before God. You don't earn His favor; you have it already. You don't outrun or overcome your sin; it has already been removed.

The Spirit lives in you, is at work in you, and is changing you! At times it can seem that you have taken two steps forward and one step back (and on bad days like you took one step forward and two steps back!), but the God who began His work in you is continually at work in you. It is all part of His work of grace in you.

It is grace that made you aware of God's love, it is grace that drew you to receive God's gift of salvation, and it is grace that stirs in you. It is a grace greater than your sin and grace more powerful than your best performance. So, my friend, celebrate that grace, grow in that grace, and rest in that grace. It is not only greater than your sin, but it is grace that will lead you home.

# NOTES

## INTRODUCTION

1.    John Newton, "Amazing Grace," 1779, https://library.timelesstruths.org/music/Amazing_Grace/.

2.    Philip Yancey, *What's So Amazing About Grace?* (Grand Rapids, MI: Zondervan, 1997), 71.

## CHAPTER 1

1.    John Wesley, letter to Charles Wesley, June 27, 1766, http://wesley.nnu.edu/john-wesley/the-letters-of-john-wesley/wesleys-letters-1766b.

2.    Augustine, *Confessions*, trans. Albert C. Outler, 1955, https://www.ling.upenn.edu/courses/hum100/augustinconf.pdf.

3.    John Wesley, journal, May 24, 1738, https://www.ccel.org/ccel/wesley/journal.vi.ii.xvi.html.

## CHAPTER 2

1.    "Acts of Paul and Thecla," in Wilhelm Schneemelcher, ed., *New Testament Apocrypha*, trans. R. McL. Wilson, vol. 2 (Louisville, KY: Westminster John Knox Press, 1992), 239, https://www.amazon.com/New-Testament-Apocrypha-Vol-Apocalypses/dp/0664227228.

2. Frederick Buechner, *Peculiar Treasures: A Biblical Who's Who* (New York: HarperCollins, 1979), 147, https://www.amazon.com/Peculiar-Treasures-Frederick-Buechner/dp/0060611413.

3. John Newton, "Amazing Grace."

## CHAPTER 3

1. Johnny Cash with Patrick Carr, *Cash: The Autobiography* (New York: HarperCollins, 1997), 169–71, https://www.amazon.com/Cash-Autobiography-Johnny/dp/0060727535.

2. Holley Gerth, *Fiercehearted: Live Fully, Love Bravely* (Grand Rapids, MI: Revell, 2017), 31.

3. Robert Farrar Capon, *Between Noon and Three: Romance, Law, and the Outrage of Grace* (Grand Rapids, MI: William B. Eerdmans, 1997), 109–110, https://books.google.com/books?id=PyoS2iO64ugC&q.

## CHAPTER 4

1. Francis Spufford, *Unapologetic: Why, Despite Everything, Christianity Can Still Make Surprising Emotional Sense* (New York: HarperOne, 2013), 42, https://www.amazon.com/Unapologetic-Everything-Christianity-Surprising-Emotional/dp/0062300458.

2. N. T. Wright, *Simply Christian: Why Christianity Makes Sense* (New York: HarperOne, 2006), 4, https://www.amazon.com/Simply-Christian-Christianity-Makes-Sense/dp/0061920622.

3.    C. S. Lewis, *The Great Divorce* (New York: HarperOne, 2001), 75, https://www.amazon.com/Great-Divorce-C-S-Lewis/dp/0060652950.

## CHAPTER 6

1.    Thomas Watson, *A Body of Divinity* (West Linn, OR: Monergism Books, 2015), 281, http://www.monergism.com/thethreshold/sdg/watson/A%20Body%20of%20Divinity%20-%20Thomas%20Watson.pdf.

2.    Charlotte Elliott, "Just As I Am," 1835, https://en.wikipedia.org/wiki/Just_As_I_Am_(hymn)#/media/File:Elliott_Bradbury_Just_as_I_am.jpg.

## CHAPTER 7

1.    Henri J. M. Nouwen, *Here and Now: Living in the Spirit* (New York: Crossroad Publishing, 1994), 165, https://www.amazon.com/Here-Now-Henri-J-Nouwen/dp/0824519671.

## CHAPTER 11

1.    Martin Luther, "Large Catechism" in *The Book of Concord*, ed. Robert Kolb and Timothy J. Wengert (Minneapolis: Fortress, 2000), 428.

2.    Steven W. Manskar, *A Perfect Love: Understanding John Wesley's "A Plain Account of Christian Perfection"* (Nashville: Discipleship Resources, 2004), 41.

## CHAPTER 14

1.   Andrew A. Bonar, *Memoir and Remains of the Rev. R. M. M'Cheyne* (Edinburgh, UK: Oliphant Anderson & Ferrier, 1892), 293, https://archive.org/details/memoirremainsofr1892mche/page/292.

## CHAPTER 16

1.   John MacArthur, "Marks of a Child Adopted by God," sermon, October 26, 1997, *Grace to You*, https://www.gty.org/library/sermons-library/90-172/marks-of-a-child-adopted-by-god.

## CHAPTER 17

1.   Henri J. M. Nouwen, *The Wounded Healer: Ministry in Contemporary Society* (London: Darton, Longman & Todd, 1994), 88.

# ACKNOWLEDGMENTS

As YOU MIGHT expect, I am profoundly grateful to my heavenly Father, who has saturated my life with the evidence of His grace. He has been better to me than I could ever be to myself. If anything, these pages are a celebration of just how incredibly good He is.

Furthermore, the book you hold would not exist without the constant encouragement and creative input of my very best friend. Debbie is the love of my life; her love for me reflects God's grace and love more than anything I have known on earth.

I am also exceptionally thankful for the team members God has surrounded me with at James River Church. Their faithful support and tireless efforts are a continual source of strength. I can't imagine doing ministry without them!

Through the years many have prodded me to write. This book is, in many ways, a credit to their love, encouragement, and tenacity! Thank you.

Finally, a big thank-you goes to the Charisma team. Your partnership on this project has been a joy.